T0327027

Architecture

lost

in

and

space

Dementia

Eckhard Feddersen – Insa Lüdtke (eds.)

Architecture

lost

in

and

space

Dementia

Birkhäuser
Basel

The editors and the publisher wish to thank the following institutions and companies for their participation in this book:

BOS GmbH Best Of Steel

Mauser Einrichtungssysteme GmbH & Co.KG

Residenz-Gruppe Bremen

Hans Sauer Stiftung

Herbert Waldmann GmbH & Co. KG

Arthur Waser Gruppe

Layout, cover design
and typesetting:
Reinhard Steger
Deborah van Mourik
Proxi, Barcelona
www.proxi.me

Copy editing:
Christel Kapitzki, Berlin
Cocon Concept, Berlin

Translation from German
into English: (except for pages
86–89, 102–117, 122–133,
146–153, 164–175, 182–183
and 204–207)
Julian Reisenberger, Weimar

Library of Congress
Cataloging-in-Publication data
A CIP catalog record for this
book has been applied for at the
Library of Congress.

Bibliographic information
published by the German
National Library

The German National Library
lists this publication in the
Deutsche Nationalbibliografie;
detailed bibliographic data are
available on the Internet at
http://dnb.dnb.de.

This publication is also
available as an e-book
(ISBN 978-3-03821-120-4)
and in a German language edition
(ISBN 978-03821-467-0).

© 2014 Birkhäuser Verlag
GmbH, Basel
P.O. Box 44, 4009
Basel, Switzerland
Part of Walter de Gruyter GmbH,
Berlin/Boston

Printed on acid-free paper
produced from chlorine-free
pulp. TCF ∞

Printed in Germany

ISBN 978-3-03821-500-4

9 8 7 6 5 4 3 2 1

www.birkhauser.com

lost in space

architecture and space

individual and society

house and courtyard

block
and quarter

town
and country

prologue

Jonathan Franzen

This seems mostly right to me. By the time my father's heart stopped, I'd been mourning him for years. And yet, when I consider his story, I wonder whether the various deaths can ever really be so separated, and whether memory and consciousness have such secure title, after all, to the seat of selfhood. I can't stop looking for meaning in the two years that followed his loss of his supposed "self," and I can't stop finding it.

I'm struck, above all, by the apparent persistence of his *will*. I'm powerless not to believe that he was exerting some bodily remnant of his self-discipline, some reserve of strength in the sinews beneath both consciousness and memory, when he pulled himself together for the request he made to me outside the nursing home. I'm powerless as well not to believe that his crash on the following morning, like his crash on his first night alone in a hospital, amounted to a relinquishment of that will, a letting go, an embrace of madness in the face of unbearable emotion. Although we can fix the starting point of his decline (full consciousness and sanity) and the end point (oblivion and death), his brain wasn't simply a computational device running gradually and inexorably amok.

Where the subtractive progress of Alzheimer's might predict a steady downward trend like this –

what I saw of my father's fall looked more like this:

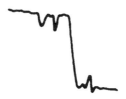

He held himself together longer, I suspect, than it might have seemed he had the neuronal where-withal to do. Then he collapsed and fell lower than his pathology may have strictly dictated, and he chose to stay low, ninety-nine percent of the time. What he *wanted* (in the early years, to stay clear; in the later years, to let go) was integral to what he *was*. And what *I* want (stories of my father's brain that are not about meat) is integral to what I choose to remember and retell.

rediscovering space

Dementia as a chance to renew our approach to architecture

Eckhard Feddersen and Insa Lüdtke

This book revisits one of the most fundamental aspects of architecture – how we perceive space – and is motivated by a consideration of how we should build for people with dementia. As the illness progresses, it causes those affected to feel increasingly lost. Until now, architecture has responded mostly by creating special buildings that attempt to compensate for the deficits resulting from a sense of disorientation. The more elementary question of how spaces can afford a sense of safety and security that contributes to greater self-assurance and a better quality of life is only rarely addressed.

The articles and projects we present in this book examine space in its different dimensions, offering answers to this question for a succession of scales and corresponding spatial constellations, ranging from *architecture and space* and *individual and society* to *house and courtyard*, *block and quarter* and the spheres of *town and country*. In all of the above, we have deliberately taken an interdisciplinary view: we asked not only architects but also gerontologists and sociologists from different parts of the world to offer their insight into current examples from research and practice. Similarly our choice of projects is not solely concerned with the problem of dementia, but rather with approaches to dealing with space that are relevant to our specific context.

Our intention with this book is to take the topic of building for people with dementia as a starting point for a wider creative renewal of the built environment that can benefit us all. Architecture that through its use of proportions, materials, light, colour and acoustics communicates elementary sensory experiences equally appeals to people with or without dementia. Buildings and spaces that engage our senses, that provide clear orientation and a sense of security and identity are beneficial for society as a whole. This approach is not just about improving the ethics and aesthetics of our built environment; it also brings economic benefits: what is good for the carers and relatives of people with dementia is also good for people with dementia – and vice versa!

For this we need interdisciplinary solutions. Dementia is more than just a diagnosis: it should be a concern of society as a whole. Not only politicians but also institutions and stakeholders such as municipalities, architects, urban planners, investors, project developers, operators of care homes as well as industry in general need to be willing to seek new directions. This book aims to set this in motion, to raise new questions and showcase possible appropriate responses.

architecture

and

space

Permeable brick façade. South Asia Human Rights Documentation Centre, New Delhi, India. Anagram Architects, 2011

learning, remembering and feeling space

Eckhard Feddersen

For people with dementia, sensory experiences play a central role. This applies especially to how we experience space. As people's cognitive faculties start to decline and the memory of recent events fades away, what remains are direct sensations. As the disease progresses, these become increasingly important. When we design architecture for people with dementia, we must therefore take a step back and consider what is fundamental about the spaces we live in. And where better to begin such deliberations than with oneself.

When I think back to my very first memory of a room from my childhood, I think of wood that smells vaguely of tar, has a pronounced grain and is warm to the touch. I was born in a wooden hut, and I lived there until I was eight years old. I see long white strips of light on a coarse sandy floor, cast by long beams resting on supports under which we played. Our hut was in a lumberyard and I remember the smell of horses and their snorting as they crossed the cobblestones. I think I felt afraid at the time. Even today, however, I still love the sensation of changing hot and cold periods in a wooden hut.

The windows in the hut were small and in winter they froze over with flowery patterns – frost flowers we used to call them – and I still like them to this day. We had no bathroom and no toilet in our barracks and instead had to use the toilets in the workmen's changing rooms across the yard. As a child I hated it, especially when the weather was stormy, which was often the case in the small town on the North Sea. Today, I still hate going outside in the dark and rain. Wooden huts with simple wood-planked walls don't have any real sound insulation. I can still hear the muffled sounds of my parents in the next room. While my actual memories of the place are indistinct, my senses – eyes, ears, nose, sense of touch – obviously played an important role in how I experienced where we lived. My sense of taste probably recorded least, but I can still remember how the ice tasted on the windows when my sister and I licked the frost on the windowpanes.

Learning space

I think my sense of space is something I have learnt. And I believe that this applies to everyone. Because so many senses are involved, this is a complicated process. As an architect, it is not surprising that one is endowed with a particularly keen sense of space or acquires this kind of sensitivity over the years. So how does one learn to appreciate spaces?

As soon as we learn to stand on two legs, our perspective changes dramatically compared to what we experienced crawling on the floor. We can cross a room more quickly, which again changes our perspective of the space as well as our physical experience of ourselves in that space. That, of course, is nothing new: we knew that long before recent advances in neurology made it possible for us to describe precisely how we cognitively perceive and comprehend spaces. Our sense of space is a projection in the mind of each of us, which is why the impression that a room makes differs from person to person. As such, the design of a room, however simple and archaic it may be, will never be experienced the same way by everyone. Space is a subjective phenomenon, not an objective fact. We try, therefore, to communicate a sense of space through its character and to describe this with the help of categories. And for the most part, we seem to be in agreement: we know what characterises a hut and differentiate it from a hall, we distinguish in similar ways between light and dark, pleasant and oppressive spaces.

Warm and comforting. The cave-like interior of the spa of the Heinrich-Schütz-Residenz in Dresden, Germany. Feddersen Architekten, 2008

In modern neurology, it is possible to accurately localise the parts of the brain responsible for the different senses, using imaging technology. We also know how information is passed to other parts of the brain via synapses. But we know comparatively little about how we can compensate for deficits caused by diseases. We know more or less that the brain can respond very flexibly when processing sensations, the formulation of speech or sequences of movement. But we still know very little about the alternative pathways that the brain uses to communicate information when parts of the brain are damaged.[1]

We must therefore fall back on insights we have into the ways in which people respond to space and the effect it produces. The most probable response that people have is what we call "normality". Otto Friedrich Bollnow wrote a most convincing explanation for this phenomenon in the German language as far back as 1961.[2] Another pioneering work from around the same time is *The Poetics of Space* written by Gaston Bachelard.[3] Both authors knew each other and commented on each other's work. Otto Friedrich Bollnow saw the house as the centre of the world and the act of dwelling as the creation of a sense of security. In the chapter on homeliness, he comes to the conclusion that the bed, along with the hearth and table are the middle of the house and therefore the most vital space for feeling safe and secure. Bachelard explores similar concerns,

especially with regard to personal well-being and the joy of dwelling. Interestingly, these elaborations on feelings and emotions from 50 years ago largely confirm the findings of recent neurological investigations.

Remembering space

If we assume that the gradual loss of senses in old age, for example as a consequence of Alzheimer's disease, proceeds in an inverse pattern to the development of the senses in infancy, we must first take a closer look at how our senses develop in early childhood.[4] We know today that our sense of taste and touch develops earlier than our sense of sight and hearing. After just two months in the womb, the first tactile nerves have formed in the fingers of an unborn child. Every experience we make leaves a trace in the brain as it grows and in turn determines how future sensations will be experienced. Our sense of sight by contrast develops slowly. Shortly after birth, newborn babies can only make out light–dark contrasts. But even at this stage, babies are able to perceive their mother's face and differentiate it from that of other people. Our sense of taste, on the other hand, is much more pronounced and the sensory cells of a baby's tongue can already clearly distinguish sweet from sour milk. Closely related to this is the sense of smell, which is responsible for some of the most powerful memories of early childhood: in their first few months, babies will already refuse food that smells unpleasant. A child's sense of hearing

The Medical Care Centre in Rothenburg, Oberlausitz, Germany, is based on a holistic understanding of health care. Feddersen Architekten, 2007

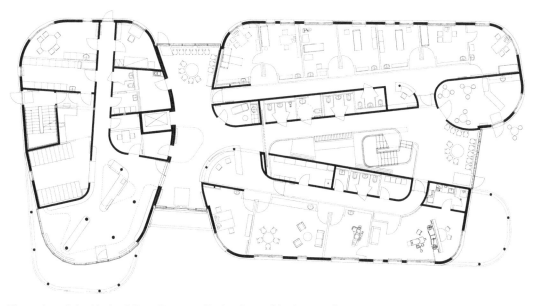

Floor plan of the Medical Care Centre in Rothenburg, Oberlausitz, Germany

Landmarks provide orientation and give public spaces a specific quality. Hammarby Sjöstad in Stockholm, Sweden. Urban development 1994–2017

Enchanting and bewildering at the same time. Piazza San Lorenzo alle Colonne in Milan, Italy

already forms while still in the womb, but only starts developing after birth. It has been shown that children who grow up with music around them develop more extensive synapses for sensing sounds in the brain. But it is in the brain that these sensory experiences are first woven together into actual impressions and sensations.

Our perception of space develops similarly. While our first experience of space begins with our bed, the blanket, the edge of the bed and the mobile dangling over our heads, one year later our perceptive faculties have developed so much that we are able to gauge distances and step by step take possession of the room we inhabit. The same applies to our first encounter with steps and changes in height, as well as the perception of light and dark areas of a room and the difference between a window and a door.

From this example, it is already clear that the most important sense for perceiving spatial characteristics and converting them into a sense of space is that of sight. Our eyes sense brightness, movement, colours and shapes at incredible speed, passing simple electrical impulses to the brain where they are assembled into images of beauty. When as designers we are called upon to imagine rooms that provide orientation and help people feel safe and happy, we therefore need consider a plethora of individual spatial characteristics that together create the desired impression.

In architectural terms, this means rooms with a clear composition that can be perceived at a glance. Spaces that turn a corner or are otherwise hard to visualise are unsettling and may cause anxiety. Large glazed surfaces as well as floor-to-ceiling windows are generally held to be attractive, but do they provide sufficient enclosure to satisfy our need for security? In corridors and communicative spaces, large-scale glazing can enliven a space and evoke positive connections, but in a room for dwelling, it should be used sparingly to avoid people feeling exposed and uncomfortable.

Feeling space

According to Bollnow, a feeling of comfort and security arises in protective environments in which we feel able to reside and move around in as we please. Only when we are at ease and shielded from hostile feelings can we fully abandon ourselves to sleep. The feeling of comfort is, however, a broader state of mind that depends on many factors, of which space is just one. The same can be said of the wish for social contact and interaction. Here too, when people go in search of conversation and friendship, they venture outside their own familiar space and open themselves to the company of others, in the process making themselves vulnerable but also happy to have stepped out of their own isolation.

The degree to which space can contribute to a general state of well-being therefore depends on the state of mind of the individual person at a given point in time. But for a room to truly evoke a particular feeling, requires the orchestration of a whole collection of specific sensory impressions, for example the pleasant smell of flowers, soothing music in the background or a nice place to sit and relax. The trend towards more sustainable architecture with ecologically-friendly and healthy building materials and a naturally regulated indoor air climate has a much better chance of creating such conditions than the technically controlled environments of the past decades. The design of these environments is pragmatic and low-tech, and focuses on the fundamental sensory qualities of architecture.

Learning, remembering, feeling – these three aspects are what makes a successful space. Planning and building for people with dementia is simultaneously an opportunity to shift our focus back to the fundamental sensory experience of architecture. It sharpens our senses for the primary and most important task of architecture: to provide shelter and enrich our lives. For this, we need to create architecture that has clear and legible qualities, that is not controlling and leaves room for alternatives. Ultimately, it is important for each of us, and especially for people with dementia, to be able to decide at any given moment where we would like to be and which spaces best meet our particular needs. This begins with whether we would like to be inside or outside; in the shelter of indoors or in the freedom of the outdoors. Even the slightest attempt at influencing this decision can be perceived as exerting control and can make people – whether or not they have dementia – feel cooped up, irritable or even angry. Only when we design both options to be equally attractive and equally easy to reach

do we respect people's wish for self-control. In my role as an architect, it is not for me to determine a desired feeling but to create opportunities for people to decide where they would like to be. This applies to the relationship between indoors and outdoors as it does for light and dark areas, for loud and peaceful rooms, hard and soft surfaces, natural and artificial materials and ultimately also for whether people would prefer to be on their own or part of the community.

For people with dementia, the availability of dual options is particularly valuable, enabling people to calm down and become themselves. One-sided options forcibly constrain an environment that for many residents is already much smaller than they are used to. A variety of spaces gives people the freedom to live their own lives in harmony with others and creates a basis from which people can get to know each other. Every resident had previously led another life, each of them has different memories and each of them feels something special. We can only cater for this with architecture that provides different and complementary options. We need to create spaces in which people can live how they have learned to live, in which memories can find a home and in which feelings find an echo. This is how we can do justice to people – whether or not they are affected by dementia.

1 S. E. Schultz and J. A. Kopec, "Impact of chronic conditions", in: *Health Reports* 14 (2003), 4, pp. 41–50.

2 O. F. Bollnow, *Human Space*, translation C. Shuttleworth. London 2011.

3 G. Bachelard, *The Poetics of Space*, translation M. Jolas. New York 1964.

4 S. E. Schultz and J. A. Kopec, op. cit.

Local materials and a strong connection to the outside world make this a comfortable and appealing interior for all the senses. Villa Mairea in Noormarkku, Finland. Alvar Aalto, 1939

people, space and context

In 1929 when Oskar Schlemmer left the Bauhaus Theatre at the Bauhaus Dessau, founded in 1921 by Walter Gropius, he wrote in his diary: "One should have deep respect and deference for any action performed by the human body, especially on the stage".[1] The "Bauhaus dances" that were developed at the Bauhaus Theatre Workshop between 1926 and 1929 examined the relationship of the body to space and how it can shape the fundamental characteristics of space through form, colour, sound, movement and rhythm. The Bauhaus Dancers continue to fascinate artists around the world to the present day, as seen in the choreographic work of the Taiwanese dancer Yun-Ju Chen. She is convinced that these historical studies of movement combined with modern-day physical exercises and self-discovery methods could contribute to improving the spatial perception of people with dementia. The image on the left is from the THEATER DER KLÄNGE Düsseldorf – production "Figur und Klang im Raum", 1993.

1   Diary entry of May 1929, see Tut Schlemmer (ed.), *Letters and Diaries*, Stuttgart 1977.

architecture should be self-evident and comprehensible

An interview with Volkwin Marg

V. Marg: Architecture and dementia is a hot topic at present. We have just completed a vast laboratory building for interdisciplinary gerontology at the University of Cologne with space for 60,000 mice and 400 researchers. The entire facility is just for research into ageing. Opposite the CECAD building, as our facility is called, a second similar laboratory is being built for the Max Planck Society, housing a further 40,000 mice. That means that in Cologne alone, experiments are being conducted on nematodes, fruit flies and 100,000 mice. This is currently how we respond to society growing ever older.

Yes, and this is motivated by the so-called demographic factor, which concerns us at many levels. If we consider, for example, contemporary architecture – which, of course, can take many different forms – can you see how it is responding to these changes?
V. Marg: Architects themselves are a good example: the majority of them do not live in the kinds of interiors that they design for others but choose to live in existing, often old buildings that appeal to their emotional sensibilities. The design of housing needs to create a sense of homeliness that satisfies the basic and fundamental needs that we associate with living. We're not talking here about home design and styling fashions. Our living requirements have developed over thousands of years and for the most part transcend fashion-oriented consumer trends.

What do you mean then by "basic and fundamental needs"?
V. Marg: How we live – whether in a cave, igloo, tent, bamboo hut, stone house or a fully air-conditioned high-rise – is in essence still a primal experience that is anchored in one way or another, depending on how we grew up, in our subconscious. It is a legacy of man's early archaic way of living and sets us apart from other primates. As individuals, each of us relives the various superimposed stages of consciousness, just as mankind does collectively. In a biological context, we are familiar with this through embryonic development.

How should we imagine these superimposed stages of consciousness?
V. Marg: In his celebrated book "The Ever-Present Origin", the philosopher Jean Gebser differentiates between four stages of the evolution of human consciousness. This first is magic, the second mythical, the third rational and the fourth, which he says we are currently experiencing, is the integral. One can think of this cumulative acquisition of habitual patterns as analogous to the programming of a computer medium with successive layers of information. When our hard disk is full with a lifetime's worth of living and other experiences, it can transpire that these layers begin to detach, from top to bottom, i.e. they fall away chronologically from the end to the beginning.

Which brings us to the subject of dementia …
V. Marg: Sooner or later, each of us will experience this path back to our original sensibilities to a greater or lesser degree. When we first begin to lose our memory, it is usually the most recent layer that starts to disappear, i.e. our short-term memory. We don't need a doctor to know that! Our long-term memory persists for longer, but when that starts to fade what remains is the disposition that we inherited from primeval times and that is still embedded in our subconscious: What do I need to feel safe? To feel good? What satisfies my innermost sensory needs? Do I feel warm? Am I being soothed? What do I feel, even when I no longer understand what is being said?

What implications does this have for architecture? You often talk about the scenography of space. What does that mean in the context of design and building?

V. Marg: In the same way that we sometimes speak metaphorically of the stage on which our lives play out, our built surroundings also constitute a form of architectural scenery. Architects design the backdrop for everyday life, except that here the backdrop remains standing for generations, even when what goes on within their walls changes over time.

How do we perceive space – as an image or as something we physically experience? And what role does memory play in this?
V. Marg: We experience space both physically and with our senses. In our memory, the image we have of a space serves as a kind of stenograph that exists alongside our earlier sensory experience and helps us to recall it.

In your article on "Interior Design" you write: "While preparing the interior for use by my mother, I disregarded everything that

Whether in a cave or a skyscraper, dwelling, as a legacy of man's earliest way of living, is still about serving our most primal needs for shelter.

Different-sized apartments cater for varied individual living requirements. Collegium Augustinum in Hamburg, Germany. gmp Architekten, 1993

in my profession as an architect I had learnt about outward appearances." What do you mean by that?

V. Marg: Working as an architect is always a learning experience. For me, this was especially so in the design of the Collegium Augustinum in Hamburg, which contains a range of different-sized apartments for 130 residents. My mother's move from her large 4-room apartment in an old building in Lübeck to a small apartment in the Collegium Augustinum taught me how vital it is for people to find familiar aspects of their living environment and the ambience of how they have lived for much of their lives in miniaturised form in a new, smaller apartment. On moving in she exclaimed: "How lovely, it reminds me of home!" She hadn't originally intended to move, but she felt at home in the new surroundings and not as if she had been transplanted elsewhere. I suspect that she would not have felt the same about other people's architectural visions – including my own.

Despite the fact that people gradually venture out of their homes less and less as they grow older, shouldn't we also endeavour to accommodate the needs of people who, for example, have cognitive difficulties perceiving space in other kinds of buildings?

V. Marg: Designing for people with (age-related) disabilities is by no means limited solely to their immediate four walls. One can accommodate physical disabilities, for example when people have trouble seeing or walking, restricted mobility or simply poor orientation, using a range of aids but also by employing simple, straightforward building details.

Barrier-free building does, of course, have natural limits. Figuratively speaking, one cannot simply level the Alps. Consequently, one should always weigh up in which situations, for whom and to what degree such measures are appropriate.

And how can architecture compensate for cognitive disabilities?

V. Marg: Very easily: by designing buildings to be self-evident and straightforward. That approach is also good for people without disabilities. The best architecture, whether complex or simple in its spatial configuration, should be self-evident to use. Signage and wayfinding systems, whatever form they may take, cannot be more than an aid and are often only partially effective, even for people without cognitive difficulties.

That is precisely the question. Do we really need something different – or can we use existing means to improve orientation?

V. Marg: That brings us back to an old issue. I suspect you are trying to provoke me a little here, but I am very, very sceptical that when you change buildings and technical instruments, there will actually be users who make use of them. What we really need is a change in social consciousness – which brings me to the actual crux of the matter: we have experienced a lifespan in which "Me, me, me …" and "I have a right to …" have predominated. A generation has grown up believing that care for the elderly is not a personal matter but the responsibility of the state. This degeneration of social consciousness is something that architecture cannot compensate for.

The interview was conducted by Christel Kapitzki and Insa Lüdtke.

Sigrid Sandmann: "gewohnt" (habitual), part of the "Kanalisierung" (Canalisation) art installation. C15 Collection Ulla and Heinz Lohmann, Hamburg, Germany, 2009

change of scenery: one space – different impressions

An interview with Friederike Tebbe

Ms Tebbe, in your work you use the term "colour biographies". What do you mean by that?

F. Tebbe: This is a central aspect of my work on the subject of *colour and memory*. As humans, we are able to differentiate between some eleven million different shades of colour, but we can only identify on average around eight to ten colours. Because we experience colours with our senses, to describe them we rely on analogies and associative terms that we have connected with our impressions of a colour and retained in our mind's eye. These inner images are memories; they serve as our archive of colours, as a collection of colour impressions that we refer to when talking about colours.

Unlike forms, we do not perceive colours as something complete. We don't grasp them intellectually in their entirety; we sense them as an idea. Our collective context and personal sensibilities play a key role in the place, connotation and value we accord to colours. *Flashback* is an intervention of mine that takes the form of a test in which you can explore your own personal collection of colour impressions, allowing you to trace your memories, recall your inner images and in effect explore your own colour biography. Because this approach is concerned primarily with how we habitually see things, it also serves as a useful basis for developing colour concepts.

How do you go about designing a colour concept for an interior? Do you see these colour histories as a kind of "layering"?

F. Tebbe: For me, the aspect of layering features in the design of spaces is as follows: to begin with there is the hardware – the configuration of the space, its floor plan and the proportions of the room. Then there are the visible surfaces, e.g. the materials of the floor, ceiling, walls, windows and doors, such as wood, plaster, concrete etc. I often find that people first consider colour at a very late stage, as if it were just an element of decor to be added when all else is finished, but the design of colour concepts actually begins much earlier with the selection of materials, as wood, metal and concrete have quite different colours. And then we should not forget that there is, of course, light which plays a vital role in how we perceive colours and the impression they create.

The next aspect is that of function: how and by whom is the space used, what needs to be emphasised and what should recede into the background. A key question is how one should feel in this space. In this context, I see my work as an act of translation: through the use of colour, I help to adequately represent what takes place in a space or a sequence of spaces.

What role do textures and light play in how they interact with colour?

F. Tebbe: Light and the surface on which it falls must be considered in conjunction with one another as they both play an important role in how colours appear and thus the impres-

Colour scheme for the function rooms and offices. Conversion. Berliner Dom in Berlin, Germany. Friederike Tebbe, 2013

Colour scheme for the dining room of Villa C in Munich, Germany. Friederike Tebbe, 2011

Colour concept for the interiors of the Kompetenzzentrum für Menschen mit Demenz (Competence Centre for People with Dementia), Nuremberg, Germany. Friederike Tebbe, 2006

sion they make. A red glass surface does not look the same as a red fabric curtain. Although essentially one and "the same" colour, they are perceived quite differently due to the different textures. A change in texture gives a colour a different energy, and can be used to create shifting landscapes of colour. There are lots of different ways in which one can play with the changeability of colours in the design of interiors.

Talking of "playing", what is your opinion on the "scenographic design" of interiors?

F. Tebbe: I see the scenography of a space as how it presents itself. In terms of the architecture, this begins with the choice of materials for the visible surfaces. The scenographic backdrop is so to speak the surfaces and how they are seen, heard and felt. While a nicely decorated room may consist of many small touches, it is ultimately no more than that. The successful scenographic design of a space on the other hand changes how the room is perceived as a whole.

This aspect is particularly relevant in the design of buildings such as hospitals and care homes. Here different cultural tastes must take a back seat: the creation of a sense of safety and well-being is of foremost importance. In this kind of atmospheric design of interiors, the use of colour and materials is especially challenging, but it also offers great scope for creativity. While the physical structure of a space remains unchanged, its atmospheric presentation – its scenography – varies. As such it is able to adapt to different uses.

What conclusions do you draw from your approach to designing with colour in the context of "old age"?

F. Tebbe: The ability to tap into biographical aspects is especially relevant in the context of designing for people with dementia. Here design and styling is not so much about creating successful aesthetic compositions but about creating surroundings and living environments that impart a sense of familiarity. Stimulation is also an important aspect of such spaces. In this case, scenography satisfies a need by means of pretence: the impression of a space that communicates a sense of warmth and security. In old age, the need to feel safe and secure is of primary importance. That means places that are easy to find one's way around and that impart a sense of security – and not the schematic signage and wayfinding systems we are usually accustomed to in hospitals. In my view, colour can play a vital role in strengthening, or even engendering, an atmosphere of security and well-being. This is not achieved by simply applying colour to a few walls but rather in the harmonious composition of forms and textures and colours and surfaces, using curtains, furniture and lighting as well as paintings on the walls. The use of typical local materials such as brick or wood, can, for example, help link a place to its regional context. But here too, less is often more. While the careful accentuation of individual items and places is good, so too is the principle of reduction helpful in ensuring that people have a clear overview of where they are.

The interview was conducted by Insa Lüdtke.

A succession of colours in the entrance hall, kitchen and corridor of Villa C in Munich, Germany. Friederike Tebbe, 2011

Colour scheme for the conversion of a town house in Braunschweig, Germany. Friederike Tebbe, 2012

sonnweid house

Extension of a nursing home

Wetzikon, Switzerland

Architects and interior designers
Bernasconi + Partner Architekten AG, Lucerne, Switzerland

Client
Krankenheim Sonnweid AG, Wetzikon, Switzerland

Planning
2006–2012

Completion
01/2012

A central feature of the third new extension to Sonnweid Nursing Home is its internal circulation concept based around a ramp system that enables residents to safely reach all levels on foot. The stairs are used only by staff or in the event of a fire. The entire building is organised around the ramp, a conspicuously designed element in the centre of the building, which forms part of a movement concept that continues outside as a circular route through the garden and is part of an "endless loop" that allows residents to safely exercise their urge to move around.

The ramp incorporates the elements of fire, water, earth and light as sensations in an abstract form. As such, it becomes an interactive element presenting residents and visitors ascending or descending the ramp with visual, tactile and acoustic stimuli. Climbing plants, a wall of water and an elephant tree serve as visual and acoustic representations of the elements, while for fire, a fuel-burning stove has been incorporated into a seating niche next to the ramp. Quotations by famous historical personages decorate the walls, with the aim of eliciting a smile. The varied arrangement of the skylights creates a changing play of light in the interior. As a result, the quality of light and its atmosphere changes as one ascends and descends depending on the incidence of daylight. Although located in the heart of the building, the ramp, like the corridors leading off it, receives sufficient daylight.

Changing vistas across and into the central space make it possible to alternately experience the elements of water and earth. The ramp is equipped with large window shutters that can be closed in the event of a fire but remain open in normal use.

Ascending ramp on the first floor

Section through the system of ramps with the elements water, earth, fire and light

33

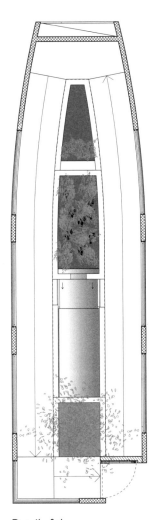

Detail of the ramp

Wall of water

The water pool and elephant tree

haaptmann's schlass

Care and nursing home for the elderly

Berbourg, Luxembourg

Architects
witry & witry
architecture
urbanisme

Client
Congrégation des
Sœurs Hospitalières
de Ste. Elisabeth

Planning
03/2005–03/2008

Construction
04/2008–07/2010

Gross floor area
7,100 m²

The "Haaptmann's Schlass" in Berbourg has metamorphosed from its original function as a home for the blind into a care and nursing home for the elderly. An extension to the existing building has been built to accommodate 72 new residents, grouped into small apartments and to serve as a new centre for the entire complex. The care home specialises in the care of people with dementia and the building was designed from the outset to accommodate their special needs such as freedom of movement, sufficient illumination and a clearly legible arrangement.

The building is situated at a step in the terrain so that it presents a single storey to the park and two storeys to the garden. From the level of the park, one reaches the restaurant area via a lift located at the junction between the existing building and the extension. The new main entrance leads directly into the various communal areas and a spacious terrace overlooking the castle park, which is the central meeting point between the existing and new building.

The 72 rooms are arranged in three pavilions grouped around a common courtyard used by all the residents. Each of the two-storey pavilions is built around a landscaped atrium and contains accommodation for twelve residents, a commun room plus kitchen, a snug and rooms for the care staff on each level. The residents' rooms are arranged around the perimeter of the pavilion and face east, south or west with views out over the surrounding countryside, while the communal areas and corridors open onto the internal atria. The small size of the residential units creates a comforting and homely sense of scale. The large-format photographs in the corridors have different themes, lending each specific area and their personal space a recognisable identity, which in turn helps residents know where they are.

Main entrance at the junction between the old and the new building

The three pavilions face onto a central, sheltered internal courtyard.

Ground floor plan of the park level of the new extension

Corridor on the first floor of the "Mosel" pavilion

Corridor on the first floor of the "Ösling" pavilion

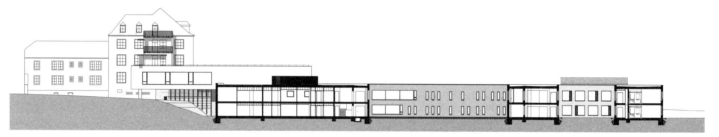

Longitudinal section through the new extension

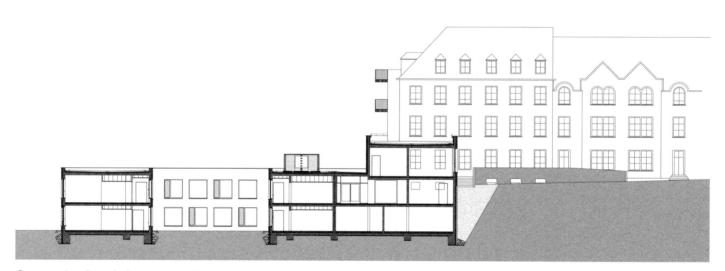

Cross section through the new extension

View of the entire complex from the surrounding countryside

house
of life

Nursing home

Solingen, Germany

Architects
Arbeitsgemeinschaft
Monse/Molnar +
Großkemm/Richard,
Wuppertal/Solingen
Stadtplaner
Innenarchitekten

Client
Drei-Alt-Solinger
Kirchengemeinden

Planning
Arbeitsgemeinschaft
Monse/Molnar +
Großkemm/Richard,
Wuppertal/Solingen

Construction
2011–2012

Completion
2013

Gross Floor Area
1,154 m²

In many cases where appropriate facilities are lacking, younger people between the ages of 18 and 65 who need regular care and are unable to live at home, find themselves living in homes for the elderly or in facilities for the disabled. What should a facility be like for people like these who in the prime of life suddenly find themselves in need of care and nursing, for example as a result of an accident or debilitating illness? The "House of Life" is a project in Solingen with a concept that offers some possible answers. Shortly after it opened, it was awarded "Project of the year 2013" by the journal *Altenheim*.

The project houses 20 young people between the ages of 18 and 60 who need regular care and is divided into three residential groups on three storeys. Colourful patterned wallpaper in the corridors and modern lamps in the communal areas create a fresh and lively atmosphere, and large and inviting dining tables evoke the community spirit of student shared housing. Residents can immerse themselves in the atmosphere of the bathroom, which has a freestanding bathtub, atmospheric lighting and a music system for listening to one's favourite music while soaking. All these reflect the very different needs of young people whether with respect to food preferences, to the structure of the day and means of communication.

The client invested a total of 2.1 million Euros in the new building, which has 20 rooms for residents. Compared with the communal areas, these have neutral colours and are comparatively small with a floor area of approximately 17 m². The private sphere of the residents was a priority for the designers and each room has its own barrier-free bathroom with sliding glass doors to increase the sense of space. As with any hotel room, each room has its own telephone and computer connection. The floor-to-ceiling windows underline the clear lines of the rectangular building, and the open character of the building corresponds to its location at the edge of the centre of Solingen. The latter is an important factor for young residents and their lifestyle, so that they are embedded in the context of friends and family. Each floor has been given a different design: the lower ground floor provides direct access to the garden and contact to nature. The floor above is more playful and baroque in character, while the upper floor has a modern and clean formal language.

The architects' design concept aims to reflect the diverse character of society as the multi-generational building houses a broad age range of inhabitants. The age of the residents is, however, not the foremost concern; the concept provides room for different ways of life that can exist in parallel regardless of age. This approach could also be promising for facilities for people with dementia as they experience different phases of their own biography during the course of the illness, but their attitude towards life remains constant.

Exterior view

Interior of level 0

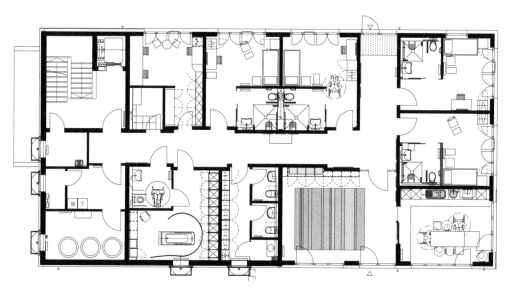

Floor plan of level 0

View along the corridor on level 2

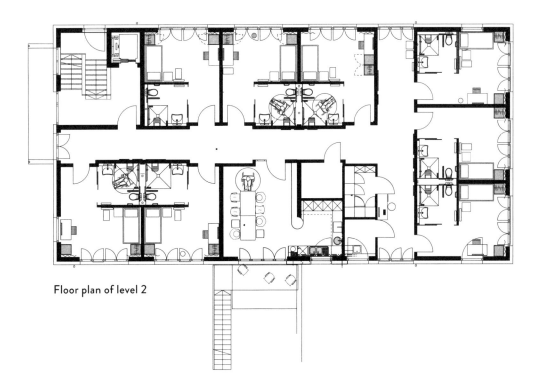

Floor plan of level 2

Corridor and dining area on level 1

View of the interior, level 2

Freestanding care-friendly bath tub in the "wellness area" on level 0

Dining room on level 0

lost

A cultural analysis of the relationship between space and dementia

Ralph Fischer

Lost really has two disparate meanings. Losing things is about the familiar falling away, getting lost is about the unfamiliar appearing.[1]

Culturally and historically, there is a close relationship between walking and thinking: the peripatetics, the followers of the school of *Peripatos* founded by Aristotle in 335 BC, were known for conducting philosophical debates while walking about. Peripatetic is derived from the word *peripatein*, which denotes the act of walking. The footfalls of walking are held to foster the development of thoughts. In various epochs in the history of philosophy, thinkers have famously walked, wandered or strolled: Jean-Jacques Rousseau, Karl Marx, Henri David Thoreau, Friedrich Nietzsche, Søren Kierkegaard were among those thinkers who went as they thought.

Method derives from the Greek word *méthodos*, which originally meant to journey after, to pursue the path to a certain goal. But to step out also means to enter into a relationship. The Latin word for step *passus* comes from *pando* which means to open, to spread. With every step one takes, the body ventures out into space. When walking, a person measures distance by the length of their strides; they test the constitution of the ground and vary their speed according to situation and context. Michel de Certeau, the French philosopher, cultural historian and general analyst of everyday life, describes the process of walking as follows: "In the framework of enunci-ation, the walker constitutes, in relation to his position, both a near and a far, a *here* and a *there*."[2] Michel de Certeau is refer-ring here to Sigmund Freud's description of a child's game with a wooden spool in his essay *Beyond the Pleasure Principle* from 1920: *The child had a wooden spool with a piece of string tied around it. It never occurred to him to drag it along the floor behind him and pretend it was a carriage, for example. Instead, he very skilfully threw the spool, attached to the string, over the edge of his little uncurtained bed so that it disap-peared therein, all the while uttering his meaningful 'o-o-o-o'. Then, using the string, he pulled the spool out of the bed again and greeted its appearance with a joyful da [there].*[3]

The child's game plays with the concepts of near and far, disappearance and appearance. In this case, the child alone determines when the object disappears and finally reappears. For Michel de Certeau, the play of steps is a direct echo of this childhood game: *To practice space is thus to repeat the joyful and silent experience of childhood; it is, in a place, to be other and to move toward the other.*[4]

There appears to be an own physical, symbolic and ontological logic to the fact that the Indo-Germanic root of the German verb "gehen" (ghe[i]), English "to go", can mean both "spread" and "step" as well as "gape, be empty, leave, to go forth". With every step, the walker balances over a gaping void. Losing his balance could quickly result in a painful fall.

Walking in endless rooms. Michal Rovner: "Current", still from video installation in the mixing works of the Kokerei Zollverein. Essen, Germany, Ruhrtriennale 2012

For many older people this is a danger that presents itself on an everyday basis. This archetypal way in which we move is in fact a highly complex procedure that we learnt with great effort in childhood and now run the risk of losing in old age as our muscles weaken. It is not by chance that the riddle of the sphinx refers to man and his forms of movement: "Tell me what this is," the riddle goes, "there is a being on earth that is four-footed, two-footed and three-footed, yet has a single voice."[5] Ironically it is Oedipus, with his swollen foot that makes him limp, who inferred that the riddle refers to man "who crawls on all fours as an infant, walks upright on two legs when grown up, and employs a stick as a third foot in old age."[6] Ancient Greek philosophy defines mankind by its gait: Ánthrō-pos, the ancient Greek word for "human" literally means two-legged. What differentiates mankind from other living beings is that he walks upright. The riddle already hints at the hurdles that space holds in store for people in old age: locomotion requires the help of a support, a prosthesis, that lends the weakened body additional stability when walking. But aside from the risk of falling over, walking can present other difficulties: the walker can lose his or her way. So, in addition to needing a walking aid to protect against falling, the walker also requires a memory aid to ensure that he does not lose his orientation in the complexities of his environment. Most people can remember from a situation in their childhood the unsettling feeling of having strayed into a strange environment without knowing the way back.

In this case the space that the person measures out with their strides does not present them with a locomotive problem but with a mnemonic problem: the walker must commit the environment to memory, must remember the path already trodden, in order not to lose his way in the expanse of space. The loss of orientation in space is one of our deepest fears. From an anthropological and mythopoetic viewpoint, it is therefore only logical that losing one's way in a foreign environment is a central theme of numerous sagas and fairy tales. In his essay on *The Uncanny*, Sigmund Freud also recounts the experience of getting lost: he describes how, while out walking in a provincial Italian town, he chances on a place in which he felt uncomfortable and from which he quickly hurries away. Freud's restless wandering through the narrow and winding alleyways brings him back to the same place three times in succession: "Now, however, a feeling overcame me," recounts Freud, "which I can only describe as uncanny, and I was glad to find myself back at the piazza I had left a short while before, without any further voyages of discovery."[7]

For many people who have dementia, this kind of experience of the uncanny can be a near-daily occurrence: the expe-rience of being a stranger in an environment that presents challenges which exceed the powers of one's own memory. In his memoir of his father, "The Old King in His Exile" (2011), the Austrian writer Arno Geiger describes how simple every-day activities and routines successively turn into irresolvable problems for his father who has Alzheimer's, with the result that the familiarity of his own home gradually gives way to a feeling of permanent alienation. As his memory disintegrates, he is left with a chronic feeling of homelessness: as one's memory continues to decline, so too does one's sense of spatial orientation. The father's walks turn into aimless meanderings, to a restless search for irretrievably lost memories. In his novel, Arno Geiger describes how the place in which his father has lived for decades gradually becomes more and more foreign:

The agonising impression of not feeling at home is one of the symptoms of the disease. To me it is as if the inner degeneration of the person with dementia causes them to lose their feeling of security and shelter and they now long to find the place where they can recover this feeling. But because the confusion they feel never ceases, even in the most familiar of places, not even one's bed can offer respite.[8]

For the father, his own home has become unknown territory. He no longer recognises the house that he himself built in the late 1950s. And so it loses its homeliness and becomes uncanny, in German *unhomely*:

Whoever was speaking, even his brethren and children, were foreign to him because what they said was confusing and unsettling. His natural conclusion that here was obviously not his home, was quite understandable.[9]

The feeling of fundamental homelessness is disturbing and unsettling. Again and again, his father wants to go home, as if by going elsewhere he can rid himself of the situation that the disease has caused.
If we are unable to dissociate "being from orientated being,"[10] as Maurice Merleau-Ponty argues in his *Phenomenology of Perception*, then the symptoms of dementia make us dramatically aware of the role of spatial structure for human identity. The person affected by dementia is confronted by a fundamental loss: when one's home environment is no longer familiar, one lives in a state of mental homelessness. At the same time, he goes in search of the place that gave him shelter before the disease took it from him: "I want to go home," says the father to his son. But he is already there, at home in his own house that he no longer recognises. And he talks to his son, who he no longer recognises as such. The course of routine gives way to aimless wandering: a restless searching with no prospect of success. He is lost.

1   R. Solnit, *A Field Guide to Getting Lost*. New York 2005, p. 22.

2   M. de Certeau, *The Practice of Everyday Life*. Berkeley 1984, p. 99.

3   S. Freud, *Beyond the Pleasure Principle*, ed. Todd Dufresne, translation G. Richter. Ontario 2011, p. 57.

4   M. de Certeau, *op. cit.*, p. 110.

5   Cf. R. Hard, *The Routledge Handbook of Greek Mythology*. London 2004, p. 310.

6   *Ibid*. p. 311.

7   S. Freud, "The Uncanny" (1919), in: *The Complete Works of Sigmund Freud*, 17. ed. by Anna Freud, translation J. Strachey. London 1955, p. 237.

8   A. Geiger, *Der alte König in seinem Exil*. Munich 2013, p. 13 (translation J. Reisenberger).

9   *Ibid*. p. 57.

10 M. Merleau-Ponty, *Phenomenology of Perception*, translation C. Smith. London 1962, p. 295.

The playful appropriation of space. Avi Kaiser, Sergio Antonino: "Carré 18" choreography, Kaiser-Antonino Dance Ensemble, The Roof Duisburg, Germany, 2012

individual

and

society

A bundle of light prevents the viewer from seeing his or her own reflection. Alessandro Lupi: "ANTIEGO mirror (identity series)", 2013

dementia as a cultural challenge

Andreas Kruse

Experiencing people with dementia reminds us of how vulnerable life is

Public awareness of dementia as a particular form of vulnerability in old age has risen significantly in recent years. This has partly to do with the fact that many people have had experience of, or are currently experiencing, the effects of this disease among members of their family, friends or neighbours and acquaintances. Because they have been personally affected, they are more sensitive to the needs of people with dementia and the kind of care this entails. Another reason is that dementia is an age-related affliction that is becoming increasingly evident in public society: almost 15 % of over-80-year-olds and almost 35 % of over-90-year-olds suffer from some form of dementia of one origin or another. Given that over the next 30 years the proportion of over-80-year-olds will rise from 6 % at present to approximately 12 %, and that we ourselves are likely to reach this old age, we become aware that we too may at some point be one of those people who suffer from dementia. When we experience people with dementia, we may also be seeing ourselves – or rather a potential fate that may befall us in future. The British writer and theologian John Donne (1572–1631) eloquently captures the challenge this presents us with – namely that of recognising one's own potential fate in what is befalling others – in *Devotions upon Emergent Occasions* (Devotion XVII) written in 1624: *Do not send to know, for whom the bell tolls, it tolls for thee."*

This seems all the more relevant when we consider that neurodegenerative dementia (most commonly manifested as Alzheimer's disease) can potentially affect all people – regardless of the lifestyle they have led – when they reach old or very old age. A further reason, finally, for the increase in public awareness is that an effective means of therapy has yet to be discovered and that the remedial effect of preventive therapy is very limited: physical and mental cognitive training can delay the onset of clinically manifested symptoms, but they cannot prevent the onset of neurodegenerative dementia.

Human dignity

A precise analysis of how people with dementia behave and experience their lives shows that the experience of belonging plays a key role in all phases of dementia for the well-being of those affected. That means that people with dementia should not be excluded from their familiar social context, but on the contrary that they should continue to be given open, sensitive and concentrated attention, even when they are no longer able to communicate verbally and our only indication of how they feel and what they want can be derived from their gestures and facial expression. This sense of belonging and the experience of open, sensitive and dedicated attention is dependent on the willingness of their social context to fundamentally respect the human dignity of people with dementia and to provide opportunities for them to actually manifest this dignity, i.e. to "live" it. For this we must consider people with dementia primarily in terms of their immediate needs and inclinations and the resources they have at their disposal rather than solely from a pathological, deficit-oriented point of view.

Where the dominant image of mankind focuses exclusively on cognitive ability, there is a risk that we may begin to think in terms of degrees of human dignity: that is as soon as a person's cognitive faculties begin to decline, their human dignity is then called into question. Numerous authors see a danger in this overly one-sided view of people for the continued open, sensitive and concentrated communication with people with dementia and for the unconditional acceptance of their person (i.e. not dependent on particular conditions or abilities). Furthermore, the predominance of this view of mankind fails to take into account the still available resources of a person with dementia, which are often of an emotional, feeling related, communicative as well as practical everyday nature. Such non-cognitive resources are just as important for personal self-actualisation – which we understand as a fundamental ability to express oneself, to communicate and to differentiate oneself – as cognitive resources. And assuming that self-actualisation is a central motive of all people, there is, in our view, a danger that an all too reductive view of mankind that focuses exclusively on cognitive ability will restrict the ability for people with dementia to realise their own potential.

Islands of the self and self-actualisation in advanced dementia
The needs that the care and assistance of dementia patients who are dying ought to fulfil require a fundamental consideration of the self and the process of self-actualisation. In order to gain a better understanding of the possible effects of emotional care and physical communication or of activation and stimulation – all central aspects of the care of dying people with dementia – we need to make fundamental assumptions about the self and the process of self-actualisation. It is these that provide a theoretical and conceptual framework for the care of dying people with dementia.

As the disease progresses to an advanced stage, the self – the coherent cognitive-emotional-motivational construct that constitutes the core of a person's personality – begins to become less and less coherent. This self is then less and less able to reflect on its relationship to itself and its surroundings, which manifests itself as a fundamental shift in how people with dementia experience their body: they begin to see their body less and less as a part of themselves and as a consequence it becomes less and less distinguishable from its environment. The result is a concomitant fundamental shift in the me-you-relationship, causing dementia patients to become increasingly fearful as they no longer feel physically protected from others.

Nevertheless, one should not overlook the fact that even when the self has lost much of its coherence in the late phases of the disease, islands of the self can still be seen: aspects of a person's personality that in earlier life were key to who they were. Existential topics that in earlier life were defining for how they experienced their world can reveal themselves again and again in specific circumstances. This shows clearly how valuable the resource-oriented perspective is when working and being with people with dementia. Similarly, a person's physical memory can still be remarkably pronounced in late stages of the disease: it has been shown that the physical memory of particular places (of high biographical significance) can persist even in late stages of the illness, providing that the care and assistance of people with dementia is oriented around continuing stimulation and activation that draws intensively on the person's biography.

Similarly, in the context of the self-determination, one can observe that, even when not visible with the same clarity as in earlier life, people with dementia are still able to sense right up into the late phases of the disease whether it is they themselves who undertake an action or another person. However, this basal form of the self-determination of people with dementia can only be experienced when the person lives in an environment in which the upholding of the me-you-relationship is made a central component of stimulation and activation, even under the aforementioned conditions of a shift in how the body is experienced.

In very advanced stages of dementia, it seems appropriate, both from a professional viewpoint as well as in terms of terminology, to speak of "islands of the self". As described above, the self can be understood as a coherent, dynamic construct comprised of numerous aspects (multiple selves) which are linked to each other (coherent) and are continually subject to change (dynamic) in response to impressions and experiences. As dementia progresses, the self loses more and more of its coherency and dynamic capacity: parts of the self are lost; existent parts of the self are less well connected; and the ability to productively adapt the self in response to new impressions and experiences is no longer active, not to mention that in advanced dementia the ability to gain new impressions and experiences also declines. But that doesn't mean that the self no longer exists: in professional contexts (both theoretical and practical), which strive to take a differentiated approach to the experiences and behaviour of patients, it must be emphasised that remnants of the self are still clearly identifiable, even in very advanced dementia. In every person with dementia – even when the disease is very advanced – there are situations to which he or she (relatively) consistently responds positively, whether contact to people with a certain charisma or attitude, or hearing a particular piece of music, sensing a particular smell, colour or sound, or when undertaking particular activities. The fact that specific situations elicit a (relatively) consistent positive reaction shows that these situations are being recognised, that they have fallen on fertile biographical land – and by the same degree that these situations speak in some way to remnants of the self.

The identification of situations that connect with positively connoted biographical experiences and therefore elicit a positive affective or emotional response has become an important component of the concept of biographical and lifeworld-oriented interventions. Especially when we assume that remnants of the self continue to exist into the late stages of dementia, this kind of individual, biographical and lifeworld-oriented approach to rehabilitation and activation is particularly useful. The core practice of this can be loosely described by the term *maieutics* (as used in ancient Greek philosophy to denote the art of assisting childbirth). Indeed, in an approach to reha-

bilitation and activation that is based on such a theory, there is a sense of "birthing", though in this case what is brought forth is biographical preferences, inclinations, likings that are expressed in "individual selves". While these no longer have the same degree of coherency, clarity and dynamic effect as they did prior to onset of the disease, they are still discernible to a certain degree. As such it is accurate to speak of remnants of the self. As shown here by the author, the conceptual approach of physical memory, when transferred to the inner situation of people with dementia, bears similarities to the assumption of the existence of remnants of the self in the advanced stages of dementia.

Caring communities – shared responsibility

The above elaborations also touch on fundamental requirements for the design of the social and spatial environment. The most general of these is the ability of people with dementia to participate in normal life. Participation in this context means much more than social integration. It denotes the possibility to actively contribute to and shape the social environment, to interact with and speak with other people, and to feel jointly responsible. With its origins in Hannah Arendt's concept of "public space", this concept of participation embraces the contribution that each person makes in their own incomparable and unique way, according to their individual personality, to shaping the common environment. This in turn requires

"It's me" – a spontaneous assertion of identity in wet paint. ter Hell: "Ich bin's", 1980

Flight and new beginning as a lasting memory. Bernd Brach: "ZusammenBruch" (Breakdown), 2006, leather case and broken glass, waxed

that the social environment be as open as possible to the individual personalities of people with dementia, to their specific forms of competence (not only in the sense of deficits but also and especially in terms of the resources they contribute), to their specific motives, interests and ways of experiencing and behaving. It also suggests the creation of *social spaces* in which people with dementia feel safe, and in which they have sufficient opportunity to creatively pursue activities of their own choosing as well as to interact with other people.

In the context of these ideas on the design of social space, calls are growing louder for a redistribution of social welfare services and for a better approach to sharing responsibility between family members, professional services and volunteers in local society. This could result in much smaller but also much more intimate and capable social networks in which it is much easier to accommodate people's creative potential – in this case that of the person with dementia. This new way of sharing responsibility could also contribute to a much more open, much less dramatic and generally more sensitive approach to how society deals with the topic of dementia. In addition, through the incorporation of (non-professional) care for people with dementia by socially committed members of society, this would contribute to effecting a shift in society back towards humanitarian ideals. This form of shared responsibility could be described as being undertaken by "caring communities", which would come together within local municipalities.

How then should we imagine these caring communities for people with dementia? There are three important components: professional care constitutes one of these and is supported by two further components: care within the family and care by socially committed members of the community. In this constellation, all kinds of care that require professional care skills would indeed be undertaken by a professional caregiver or nurse. This professional could additionally coordinate the activities that members of the family and the local community could undertake. The result would be a caring community guided by the principle of shared responsibility.

The characteristics of an age-friendly culture

1. An age-friendly culture is firstly one that includes older people in social, political and cultural discourse, and in turn in social and cultural progress. In public discourse there is a growing tendency to talk about older people instead of talking to them as people. Speaking about older people but not to them suggests that they are not seen as active and jointly responsible members of society, and that the potential they have to offer is not taken seriously. In an age-friendly culture, older men and women also have a voice and are accorded the same respect as younger men and women. An age-friendly country does not generalise about older people as a social group but respects the individual uniqueness of older men and women – and this applies equally to men and women who have dementia.

2. Related to the first characteristic of an age-friendly culture but with a slightly different emphasis is the intergenerational perspective, which represents the second characteristic of an age-friendly culture: old age constitutes an integral part of an intergenerational perspective in which – and this is supported by empirical studies – there is an active exchange of ideas, knowledge, experience, assistance and goodwill between generations. The inclusion of old people in this exchange between generations represents an important means of participation for older people, and more so than for younger people – and this applies equally to those men and women who have dementia.

3. An age-friendly culture articulates a vital interest in the potential one has in old age (which can be very different from person to person) and creates conditions which promote their ability to realise their potential. This can include the creation of structures that provide opportunities such as community centres and caring communities in which different generations can come together, mutually enrich and support one another, which is an important incentive for realising one's potential in old age.

4. An age-friendly culture responds to men and women who are visibly frail or vulnerable with respect and sensitivity. It creates social spaces that promote independence and accountability and ensure the ability to participate. Examples include opportunities to interact in the local neighbourhood, a range of needs-oriented services for particular social groups and barrier-free environments that ensure that people can maintain, or regain, their sense of independence and mobility for as long as possible.

5. Should an older person have physical or mental impairments, an age-friendly culture still respects their individual uniqueness, shows respect for their human dignity, tries not to limit their quality of life through external constraints, and does not restrict their fundamental right to participation and to proper professional and ethically-grounded medical and nursing care. This culture does not grade people's degree of human dignity nor does it limit the degree and quality of medical and nursing care they are entitled to according to age: the services they receive are dependent solely on their medical indication, not their age.

6. An age-friendly culture strives to break down social inequalities among old people and to ensure that every person – regardless of education, income or social class – receives the medical and nursing care that is necessary in their respective life situation.

7. An age-friendly culture does not deny the rights, entitlements and needs of younger people, but strives to recognise and acknowledge the rights, entitlements and needs of all generations without favouring or disadvantaging any particular generation. This applies especially with regard to the design of the structure of the social welfare and health care system.

tools for remembering

"Nuts on Circles" is an interactive tool comprised of a series of individual objects that have biographical links to people with dementia – in this case a technically-minded organic farmer. The designer Annina Gähwiler developed a prototype in 2013 consisting of a brass axle onto which individual abstract pieces can be threaded much like nuts and bolts. Bright colours, contrasting materials with different haptic qualities (wood, metal, artificial resin/silicon, hide, cow's horn and felt) along with graphical engravings stimulate the senses and emotions of the user. The tool invites the user to move and twist the elements, creating clicking noises. This physical activity stimulates procedural memory, helping the user to reinforce the memory of knowing how to perform a certain task.

dementia – forms, research and prognoses

Bente Heinig, Markus Zens
and Elisabeth Steinhagen-Thiessen

Dementia describes a disorder in which the progressive deterioration of cognitive faculties ultimately leads to a loss of the competencies one needs in everyday life. This is sometimes accompanied by non-cognitive disorders in the form of apathy, depression, aggression, sleep disorders and delusion, which are often a considerable burden for the patients themselves as well as their relatives.

Forms of dementia

When talking about the affliction in general without referring to a particular form of the disease, "dementia" is the best term to use. The term "Alzheimer's disease" is commonly but incorrectly used to denote all forms of dementia. The most common forms of dementia are:

1. Alzheimer's disease
2. vascular dementia
3. mixed dementia (Alzheimer's and vascular dementia)
4. Alzheimer's disease and Morbus Parkinson
5. dementia with Lewy bodies
6. frontotemporal dementia
7. morbus Parkinson
8. Creutzfeldt-Jakob disease
9. other forms of dementia

As there is no categorical biochemical marker for the disorder, the currently available means of diagnosis can only search for indications. Similarly, the boundary between the normal process of age-related cognitive decline, milder forms of abnormal cognitive impairment and the beginnings of dementia are blurred. The most important forms of dementia are:

Alzheimer's disease

This is the most common form of dementia and is caused by progressive degeneration and death of the synapses and nerve cells in the hippocampus and cerebral cortex, the reasons for which are not fully understood. There are, however, various risk genes (gene variants) that are associated with an increased risk of developing dementia, for example apolipoprotein E4. Symptoms typically start to appear around the age of 65.

Vascular dementia

This type of dementia is attributed to a prevention of normal blood flow to the brain as a consequence of damaged blood vessels. High blood pressure in middle age is a known risk factor for vascular dementia, as are diabetes mellitus, lipometabolic disorders and smoking.

Worlds for people in all their uniqueness. Tamara Kvesitadze: "Relationship", Art Biennale, Venice, Italy, 2011

Moving fluorescent elastic bands in a dark room create a sense of disorientation. Gianni Colombo: "Spazio elastico", 1967

Dementia with Lewy bodies

This form of dementia can occur in its own right (primary symptom) as well as a secondary symptom of Parkinson's disease. Characteristic for DLB are fluctuations in cognition, visual hallucinations and uncontrolled movements.

Frontotemporal dementia

As the name suggests, this form of dementia affects the frontal temporal lobes and prefrontal cortex of the brain. Many patients develop a gradual breakdown in speech fluency. This can be accompanied by difficulties with naming and word comprehension and sometimes a change in social behaviour and loss of inhibition.

Research and therapy

Over the past few decades, intensive research has been conducted into the different forms of dementia but the causes have still not been fully clarified. As far back as 1998, the Nun Study showed that women whose brains exhibited large quantities of the beta-amyloid plaques associated with Alzheimer's are still able to undertake extraordinarily complex activities.

These findings have had consequences for research into suitable therapies. When the presence of amyloid plaques as evidence of cognitive impairment is no longer seen as a reliable indicator of dementia, therapy should not focus exclusively on reducing their occurrence. For the therapy of dementia, it is vital to attribute the exhibited brain function impairment to a corresponding form of dementia, which is, as described above, not always categorically possible.

The first step is to exclude or treat reversible causes such as Vitamin B12 deficiency or hyper- or hypothyroidism. Risk factors that cause damage to blood vessel can be minimised by making changes to one's way of life (e.g. through sport, losing weight, stopping smoking) as well as with certain medication (e.g. blood pressure reduction and lipid-lowering medicines). Depression can also exhibit similar symptoms to the development of dementia, so the need for proper diagnosis is important.

A range of different therapy approaches using medication are available but until now the results have been relatively disappointing. There is to date no causal therapy. Anti-dementia agents (for example acetylcholinesterase inhibitors) can only ease the effects of the symptoms but are unable to stop or slow down the degeneration of the affected brain structures. However, an American study was able to show that treatment with the acetylcholinesterase inhibitor

donepezil prolonged the period in which people were able to live without needing to enter a care facility by an average of 21.4 months. Freely available ginkgo-based preparations for the prevention and treatment of Alzheimer's disease remain as popular as ever, although their effectiveness has never been confirmed in studies.

Prognoses and outlook

The table below provides an overview of the incidences of dementia in different populations in 2010.

	People with dementia in 2010
worldwide	35.6 million (all dementias)
Germany	1.4 million (all dementias)
USA	4.7 million (only Alzheimer's)

Source: own compilation based on data from the German Centre of Gerontology (DZA), the World Health Organisation (WHO) and Hebert et al.

A current U.S. study estimates that by the year 2050, 13.8 million people will suffer from Alzheimer's in the USA alone if no preventive measures are developed before then. At present, despite intensive research, there is no causal therapy available for dementia. All we can do with currently available medication is to prolong the period before the loss of everyday competencies sets in. In addition to all of the above, patients with Alzheimer's should receive other kinds of (non-medicinal) therapy, for example strategies for helping them recall the information that they can still access, for maintaining their physical resources for as long as possible as well as psychotherapeutic support. They need an environment that provides easy orientation and care staff trained in the care of people with dementia. Likewise, it is important to more actively incorporate as well as support family members and relatives, who are also stressed by the illness.

dementia – an illness with many repercussions

Interdependencies between the family, care services, caregivers and residents

Michael Schmieder

"Mum's going to have to go into a home," announces the daughter to her family on returning from hospital. This has a knock-on effect on everyone: the patient's husband, the two daughters and the son, each in their own way. For years the daughter has done her best to take care of her mother, although she can't deny it has tried her patience. Her own marriage has suffered as a consequence of her mother's growing dementia and she and her husband don't talk like they used to. Her children visit less frequently than before as they find it hard to come to terms with their grandmother's descent into dementia. But now the days of home nursing look they will soon be over. But what about their grandfather – he's also not as compos mentis as he once was. What will happen to him when Mum goes into a home? And anyway: who's going to pay for it all? Her brother? He lives far away and runs his own company. He can't bear the sight of old people wasting away: he's so afraid of it that he'd rather take his own life before he gets that old. Then again, their parents gave him the money he needed to start his company; it was supposed to be a secret but of course everyone knows. And now they really need that money: homes are expensive. Her sister is not much help either: she lives in the country living her dream – or nightmare depending on how you see it – of a green life with only the few things she really needs. Her response: "Stay cool, no need to get stressed about it …"

Dementia always affects an entire system. Only one person is ill, but many are affected. As the example above shows, a whole series of questions arise, many of them of an existential nature, that can have far-reaching consequences. How will things change at home? How will the patient fare in the care home? Can the home provide the necessary care? And, who's going to pay for it all?

The first signs of the problem typically begin a few years earlier, but for a while the surroundings are able to adapt accordingly as the mental faculties of the affected person decline – most families are still fairly robust and able to deal with things. Direct help is often not sought at this stage, due to the much-vaunted mobility of our society. An ever-growing range of outpatient care services takes care of what was once the responsibility of the extended family and relatives. And they have a vested interest that the patient continues to "get along fine" at home for as long as possible. Sometimes, however, not everything is quite as "fine" as people make it out to be. Neighbourhood help schemes can offer real help and give structure to the week and routine to everyday life, but they can also be a strain. Things commonly held to be beneficial, such as some memory training exercises, may end up confronting people with what they are no longer able to do. A range of

Carers need to be particularly patient and professional when dealing with the so-called "challenging behaviour" of people with dementia.

day care programmes and afternoon teas with bright sounding mottos such as "care with a song" do their best to ensure that people remain active as they descend into dementia, offering opportunities to play games and sing together.

The received wisdom that "outpatient care takes precedence over inpatient care" blindly assumes that being at home is better than being in a care home: it doesn't matter whether the work is done well or not, or whether the care staff coming through the door are competent, caring or neither of these – if the family doesn't witness it, they won't know any better. Grandmother's complaints go unheeded, because it's hard to imagine that Sister Inge can be so heartless.

The practice of "caring for one another" needs people, and needs the social recognition that we function as a community, that one's home environment doesn't end at the front door but extends further and further into the local quarter or district. Only once we have embraced this can we develop corresponding local concepts that can be more than a place to meet in the local community centre or similar institution.

For many, a care home is a last resort: "We've failed her. Now we've got to bring her where she never wanted to be!" When patients move into a care home, it is true that they leave a social network, but they also enter another. That's not easy for everyone involved. For years, a nursing home was seen as the last option – "outpatient care is better than inpatient care" – and now the family must concede defeat. What kind of people work in such places, and what brings people to work there at all, given that nursing homes are accorded a place at the bottom of the hierarchy of care services? To constantly know that what one does is accorded little social recognition, that it is perceived as being little more than changing incontinence pads and washing patients, that there is always more than one can manage to do no matter how hard one works – all this has effects on an entire system – this time that of nursing care. And should the dementia patient actually start to feel better in the company of others in a nursing home where they are no longer constantly confronted by their own inadequacies, a common and equally unflattering response is that there was no more that the family could have done for the respective person – they are now better off in the care of a nursing home than in their own home.

The environment we live in is important, and the relationships we have are vitally so. They both form the basis for all the care concepts that we develop, whether outpatient or inpatient. It is no surprise, then, that architecture can play a central role,

Moving to a home can often free people from feeling confronted with their own declining cognitive faculties. Gustav U., Photographs "Später Besuch" (Late Visit), 2008

A recreated "front room" in a care home helps ease the transition and encourages residents to maintain social contact.

because the environment can be designed. To enable social interaction, our environment must be conceived and planned accordingly: What takes place in a nursing home? What needs to be made possible, and what should not happen? Who should it relate to, and how? This is not referring to the kinds of adaptations we make to our own homes – those are primarily about making the environment "conducive for caring". Architecture begins at the scale of the local neighbourhood, by promoting the urban development of cities for people in general, not specifically for people with dementia. The US gerontologist Julie Bessant Pelech argues that "designing for people with dementia is no different from designing for everyone," and outlines a view of architecture that focuses on the needs of people, one that makes connections in order to allow people to develop relationships more easily. She calls on architects to do their utmost to ensure that all the participants involved in the respective processes work together to create an environment that really works and not simply to apply preconceived systems. What we need is an aesthetic understanding that provides enough space to simply be, to be able to wander about it without feeling hemmed in by boundaries. And if we can provide this space with more than the very basic necessities, the result is an architecture that speaks directly to those who use it.

Indoors, outdoors and in-between

The task we are faced with is to connect these three zones and to make movement between them as easy as possible. Indoor areas need to provide plenty of communal space as people in an advanced stage of the disease tend to walk about a lot in public areas, and not in private. It is important for them to be part of a community and to have the opportunity to make chance contact with people. Zones are needed that allow people to move around without obstruction, that offer places to sit down, that are stimulating on the one hand and relaxing on the other, that facilitate verbal as well as non-verbal communication, that promote sensory perception and feature attractions that we associate with positive emotions.

Architecture has the potential to engender incredible possibilities, though it need not be in the form of special kinds of buildings for people with dementia but through buildings for people in general. The ability to enjoy an aesthetically pleasing space does not depend on a particular diagnosis. There are,

of course, aspects that need special attention, such as the clear legibility of rooms, and the careful design of wet areas etc. The lighting should be designed to cater for the needs of people in old age and not especially for those with dementia. In-between spaces – e.g. covered terraces, conservatories or glazed atria as well as other semi-outdoor areas protected from wind and weather – are particularly valuable spaces because they extend the period of time in which people are not forced to reside indoors, and because they extend the indoor environment that we can experience and occupy.

Outdoor areas should enable people to move around freely, to spend time and savour the pleasure of being outside. The design of such spaces should emphasise what we typically value about the outdoors. Every garden should stimulate the senses with blossoming flowers and growing trees, so that people can experience themselves as a part of nature.

It is a fact that people with dementia gradually lose their cognitive faculties. In light of this, we should perhaps also ask ourselves why we try so hard to maintain these faculties. Might it not be better to channel our energies into designing our surroundings in such a way that the loss of these faculties is not perceived as a loss, but as a transition into a new state. The less we need to rely on cognitive faculties to cope with everyday activities, the easier it will be to lead a relaxed and capable life. As harsh as this may sound, it does make clear that by wanting to maintain our cognitive faculties for as long as possible, we cause considerable stress, not only for those that are healthy but particularly for people with dementia. The task we face, and the task that architecture must address, is to cater for the needs of people rather than the illness, and to do all that is possible to enable them to live a normal human life. Architecture forms a framework within which interrelationships and social life can be made easier, and which connects the indoor realm with the world outside. In this context, care homes can be seen as an extension of the front room of the family house, a place in which interactions with family and friends can take place in familiar surroundings. And last but not least, the creation of aesthetically pleasing, well-designed surroundings helps caregivers perceive themselves as part of an environment in which they also feel valued.

alzheimer's – fate or challenge?

Wolf D. Oswald and Monika Wachter

According to what we know today, it seems almost certain, even inevitable, that in future a large number of people will develop Alzheimer's in old age. Does this mean that this is our fate: that it is unavoidable and impossible to prevent? At the same time, many see Alzheimer's as the greatest challenge facing society today. Why? There are a variety of reasons for this:

Due to the increase in life expectancy in Germany, we can expect to see a steady increase in the number of people with dementia. In a retrospective study of people who had died, evidence was found of dementia in up to 50% of 85-year-olds [1] (Fig. 1).

It is fair to assume that in more than 90% of all cases of dementia, Alzheimer's disease is the primary form, even when in 30% of these cases it is accompanied by changes to blood vessels in the form of vascular or multi-infarct dementia. One way or the other, Alzheimer's always leads to a loss of independence and everyday competencies and eventually the need for constant nursing care. A Canadian study [2] from 2003 as well as a more recent German study [3] show that Alzheimer's, a stroke and incontinence are the main reasons why people eventually need constant care. Of these, Alzheimer's accounts for the majority of cases (Fig. 2).

At the same time there will be ever fewer people who can take care of us. In 1875, for every 75-year-old, there were 95 younger people who could potentially take care of him or her. In 2008, there are now only 10.6 younger people. By the year 2050, it is estimated that this number will sink to just 3.9. [4] Our current system of care for the elderly will be hard pressed to fulfil its role at all, given the projected lack of staff (Fig. 3).

In view of these developments society urgently needs to examine how we can implement processes, using suitable preventive measures, that can help improve cognitive functioning, and with it independence and personal competency, for as long as possible, or even to delay the onset of dementia to beyond the average life expectancy.

Fig. 1: Results of a retrospective study of deceased persons showing the proportion of people who suffered from dementia in the final stage of their lives grouped by age of death

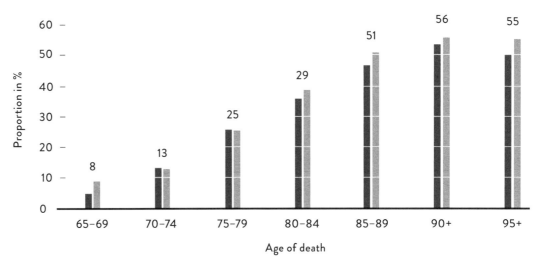

Fig. 2: The need for long-term nursing care – which illnesses pose the greatest risk?

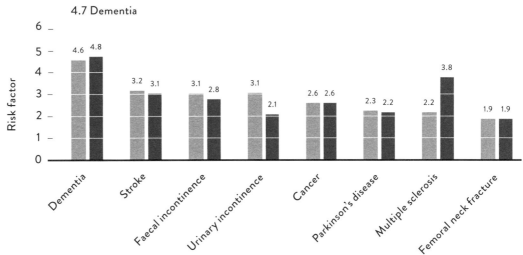

Men   Women

Several studies confirm a significant link between the occurrence of dementia and a person's earlier level of education and their degree of intellectual and physical activity.[5,6,7] One possible explanation might be that people who were more highly taxed mentally in earlier life have greater cognitive reserves.[8] Several large epidemiological studies undertaken in recent years[9,10] have shown that regular mental and physical activity on an everyday basis can delay the onset of Alzheimer's – and with it the resulting need for care – by several years.[11]

Findings of the study "Conditions for maintaining and promoting independence in old age" (SimA) undertaken at the University of Erlangen-Nuremberg showed that a specific combination of memory and psychomotor training had a long-term positive effect on the retention of cognitive faculties and everyday competencies of a random sample of healthy and independent people aged 75 years or older.[12] In the 14 years since the experiment began, there have also been significantly fewer incidences of dementia in the combined training group than in other treatment groups and in the control sample.

The low incidence rate of just 10 % is all the more remarkable, given that the youngest participants at the time were already 89 years old (Fig. 4).

Parallel to the above, the study documented that deficits in cognitive performance as well as a lack of mental and physical activity were significant risk factors for the later development of dementia.[13]

All of these results confirm that mental and physical activity play an important role in delaying the onset of dementia among people in old age and that specific preventive programmes that encourage such activities can resist the premature loss of independence and everyday competencies that follow from dementia.

More detailed information of the SimA study and the training measures, together with a 14-day training programme, can be found in "Sima(R)-basic – Memory and Psychomotor Training"[14] as well as online under: www.wdoswald.de (Fig. 5).

By way of example, one of the exercises in the SimA memory-training programme is the colour-word exercise. The task consists of naming the colours of the words as quickly as possible. The time required is a measure of the person's power of concentration at that moment (Fig. 6).

An example of the psychomotor exercises involves a game with a balloon: the person is asked to propel the balloon back and forth between two hands, initially using their palms. The exercise is made progressively more difficult by alternately using fingers and changing the finger used on each hand.

A subsequent study undertaken in the context of nursing homes (SimA-P) used an activation programme specially developed for the residents of homes that was able to significantly slow the progress of dementia, even among those already affected, and halved the number of so-called multi-ple falls. The result was a highly significant reduction in the workload of the care staff (30 %) in the participating homes and a noticeable drop in staff fluctuation (14 %). This data came from the staff and patients' health records[15] (Fig. 7).

The programme's ability to slow the progress of the disease exceeded – in terms of its effect – that of all anti-dementia medication currently available on the market. This raises the question as to why huge sums of health insurance contributors' money are being spent on pharmaceuticals that have little actual effect and considerable side effects when patients could be receiving non-pharmacological activation programmes that lead to a in many ways better quality of life and longer stabilisation of everyday competencies. At the time of writing, these activation measures are not, or only insufficiently, covered by state nursing care insurance despite the fact that the benefits of non-pharmacological activation measures have been

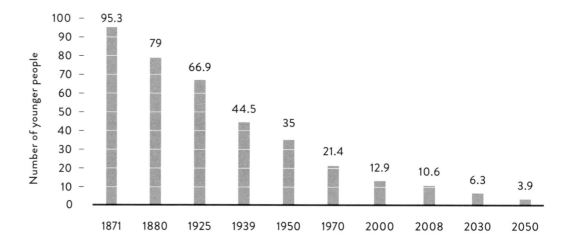

Fig. 3: Number of younger people per person aged 75 years or older in Germany

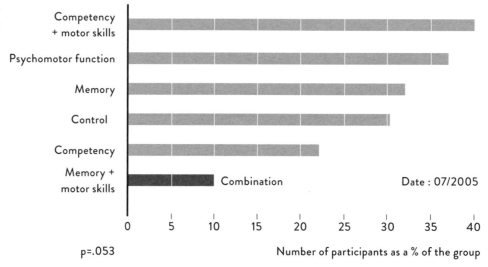

Fig. 4: Distribution of the 90 patients with dementia in the training groups

Fig. 5: Risk factors for dementia. Results of the cox regression analyses controlled for age, gender and education p<.05. Initial value N = 340 SimA participants

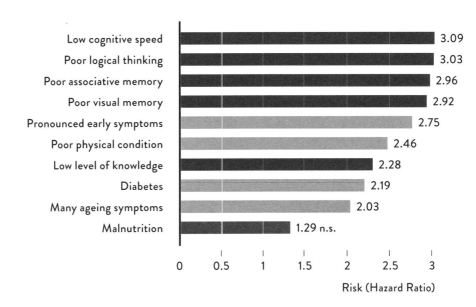

	Risk (Hazard Ratio)
Low cognitive speed	3.09
Poor logical thinking	3.03
Poor associative memory	2.96
Poor visual memory	2.92
Pronounced early symptoms	2.75
Poor physical condition	2.46
Low level of knowledge	2.28
Diabetes	2.19
Many ageing symptoms	2.03
Malnutrition	1.29 n.s.

Fig. 6: The colour-word exercise – an example from the SimA memory-training programme

red	green	yellow	blue	yellow	green
blue	red	yellow	green	blue	red
green	blue	red	green	red	blue
yellow	red	blue	red	green	yellow
red	yellow	blue	green	blue	green
yellow	blue	green	blue	green	yellow
green	yellow	blue	yellow	green	red

verified nationally and internationally.[16] Unfortunately, it would seem that Alzheimer's patients and their relatives, as well as caregivers for the elderly, have a much less influential political lobby than other interest groups in society.

It should also be noted that it has not been confirmed that a change of diet or dietary supplements have an effect on reducing the risk of dementia. This also applies to vitamin D supplements, as only about 10 % of the daily vitamin D requirement can be acquired through ingestion; the remainder being produced by the body when exposed to sunlight. Assertions to the contrary, as seen for example on the internet, are propagated entirely by companies and associations associated with the dietary supplement producers. There is, however, an increased risk of developing dementia for people with an excessively high Body Mass Index of 30 or more – the BMI is a measure of a person's weight with respect to their size (kg/m^2) –, and/or for people with poorly controlled diabetes.

In light of the dramatic care crisis ahead of us, it is hard to understand why preventive measures in Germany concentrate almost exclusively on classical illnesses such as diabetes, hypercholesterolemia and cardiovascular diseases while Alzheimer's as the number one cause for needing nursing care, is disregarded. Other countries, such as Austria, have implemented an exemplary programme of nationwide preventive measures.

One further aspect must also be mentioned: short lapses of memory or concentration are not automatically caused by dementia, and one should be careful not to prematurely assume that this is the cause. Only a professional consultation – for example as part of a "memory consultation session" – in conjunction with differential diagnostic procedures can provide a degree of certainty. Experience shows that between 10 and 30 % of the symptoms observed by dementia patients can be treated and overcome! If someone consistently emphasises his or her loss of memory, it can also be an indication of depression ("pseudo-dementia"), which is treatable. An excessive intake of medication (pharmaceutical poisoning) or dehydration (exsiccosis) due to a lack of liquids can also produce symptoms similar to that of dementia.

As described above, the fact that in future there will be far fewer young people who are able to care for the elderly needs to be seen in the context that as much as half of the population of Europe and the USA may develop dementia! If we are to mitigate the effect of the impending collapse of the care system, there is much to be said for employing non-pharmacological activation measures, especially as similar effects cannot yet be achieved through medicinal means. If it were to be possible to delay the clinical onset of dementia in Germany by up to 5 years, for example through a preventive programme similar to SimA, this could mean that some old people may die of other illnesses before they develop Alzheimer's. That in turn could reduce the number of people with dementia in our society to a level more or less equivalent to that in 2009 (Fig. 8).

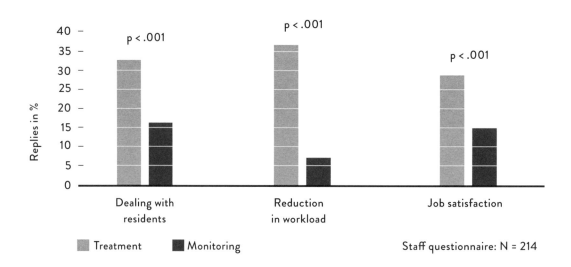

Fig. 7: Results of staff questionnaires after one year of the SimA-P activation programme

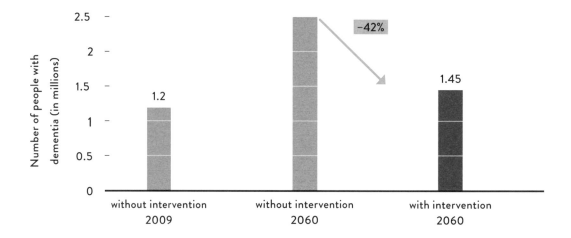

Fig. 8: Potential average annual savings in the year 2060 will amount to 50 billion Euros

1 H. Bickel, "Demenzsyndrom und Alzheimer Krankheit: Eine Schätzung des Krankenbestandes und der jährlichen Neuerkrankung in Deutschland", in: *Gesundheitswesen* 62 (2000), pp. 211–218.

2 S. E. Schultz and J. A. Kopec, "Impact of chronic conditions", in: *Health Reports* 14 (2003), 4, pp. 41–50.

3 H. Rothgang et al.: BARMER GEK, *Pflegereport 2010. Schwerpunktthema: Demenz und Pflege. Schriftenreihe zur Gesundheitsanalyse*, 5 (2010), p. 125.

4 Statistisches Bundesamt *2009, 12. koordinierte Bevölkerungsvorausberechnung* (Variante 1-W1). www.destatis.de/bevoelkerungs-pyramide/

5 M. L. Daviglus et al., "Risk Factors and Preventive Interventions for Alzheimer Disease", in: *Archives of Neurology* 68 (2011), 9, pp. 1185–1190.

6 C. R. A. Mondadori et al., "Enhanced brain activity may precede the diagnosis of Alzheimer's disease by 30 years", in: *Brain* 129, 2006, pp. 2908–2922.

7 V. N. Pavlik et al., "Influence of Premorbid IQ and Education on Progression of Alzheimer's Disease", in: *Dementia and Geriatric Cognitive Disorders* 22, 2006, pp. 367–377.

8 W. Meier-Ruge (ed.), *Der ältere Patient der Allgemeinarztpraxis, Geriatrie für die tägliche Praxis*, no. 1, 2nd ed. Basel 1988.

9 R. S. Wilson et al., "The relation of cognitive activity to risk of developing Alzheimer's disease", in: *Neurology* 69 (2007), 1, pp. 1–10.

10 D. E. Barnes and K. Yaffe, "The projected effect of risk factor reduction on Alzheimer's disease prevalence", in: *Lancet Neurol.* 10 (2011), pp. 819–828.

11 J. Verghese et al., "Leisure Activities and the Risk of Dementia in the Elderly", in: *The New England Journal of Medicine* 348 (2003), pp. 2508–2516.

12 W. D. Oswald et al., "Bedingungen der Erhaltung und Förderung von Selbständigkeit im höheren Lebensalter (SIMA).Teil XVII: Zusammenfassende Darstellung der langfristigen Trainingseffekte", in: *Zeitschrift für Gerontopsychologie und -psychiatrie* 15 (2002), 1, pp. 13–31.

13 W. D. Oswald et al., "Bedingungen der Erhaltung und Förderung von Selbständigkeit im höheren Lebensalter (SIMA). Teil XVIII: Unselbständigkeits-, Demenz- und Mortalitätsrisiken", in: *Zeitschrift für Gerontopsychologie und -psychiatrie* 15 (2002), 2, pp. 61–84.

14 W. D. Oswald, *SimA®-basic-Gedächtnistraining und Psychomotorik. Geistig und körperlich fit zwischen 50 und 100*. Göttingen 2005.

15 W. D. Oswald, A. Ackermann and T. Gunzelmann, "Effekte eines multimodalen Aktivierungsprogrammes (SimA-P) für Bewohner von Einrichtungen der stationären Altenhilfe", in: *Zeitschrift für Gerontopsychologie und -psychiatrie* 19 (2006), 2, pp. 89–101.

16 J. Olazarán et al., "Non-pharmacological Therapies in Alzheimer's Disease: A Systematic Review of Efficacy", in: *Dementia and Geriatric Cognitive Disorders* 30 (2010), pp. 161–178.

music in the therapy of alzheimer's

An interview with Dorothea Muthesius

Much research has been conducted on the relationship between music and the brain. Neurologists even suggest that music only comes about in the brain. A less scientific description is that music warms our hearts, and therefore finds its way directly to our emotions.

Dr. Muthesius, what hopes and considerations led you to employ music therapy in the treatment of people suffering from dementia?
D. Muthesius: That's not quite how it works: we didn't start out with a plan … we tried something out and then asked ourselves "Why does it work so well?" When I began working in the field of gerontopsychiatry 30 years ago, the head of department at the time was very enamoured with music and encouraged the institute's music therapist to work with our older patients. It was quite by chance that I became involved and right from the beginning I was fascinated by the experience that when I make music with people with dementia, they are – to put it simply – not ill. To feel normal, competent and healthy is an interesting experience for people with dementia – as well as for the therapist.

What form does music therapy take? Do you sing together, use rhythmic instruments, or listen to music?
D. Muthesius: It depends on the patient and his own experience. When a patient has dementia, we assume it is more important to evoke memories than to experience something new. For that we have to do a little detective work and search for what that might be. We have become specialists in reconstructing all kinds of musical biographies; and then – like any good doctor – we try out the results of our reconstruction. When we get a reaction, we continue in that direction; when there is none, we search for something else.

Is it easier if the person with Alzheimer's used to play an instrument?
D. Muthesius: No, in fact it can even be a disadvantage because if the patient was a professional musician there is much more potential for frustration. In such cases the fear of failure and perceived incompetence is stronger.

What do you do if patients do not have a particular wish?
D. Muthesius: I mostly work in institutions where the people who live there are no longer able to articulate themselves well

Singing along, clapping or dancing: music has the power to evoke emotions that in turn have a positive effect on people with dementia and their capacity to speak.

enough for us to be able to interpret a specific wish. It would, of course, be possible to work quite differently with people in the early stages of dementia, but they rarely sign up for therapy; after all, they are just at the beginning of a long process. With most of the patients I work with, I can usually tell from their reactions whether it was good for them.

And what kind of reaction do you get when you make a good choice, when you play "their song" as it were?
D. Muthesius: It very much depends on the general condition of the patient. Even when patients are bedridden and can no longer express themselves properly, one can tell if they are relaxed or excited from their breathing, as well as from their facial expression. Those who are more active may start to sing along, clap or even dance. People respond quite often with spontaneous phrases like "That was lovely" or "You brought just the right music with you". Being emotionally moved helps them to speak more lucidly.

How long do such changes last? Can the results be described, or even evaluated, in any way?

D. Muthesius: There is a scientific study that examines precisely this aspect. It shows that music therapy clearly has a significant effect and it is therefore accorded a higher recommendation grade in the S3 Guidelines for Dementia. Measurements were undertaken for a 16-week period consisting of one to two therapy sessions a week after eight weeks of treatment, after 16 weeks of treatment and four weeks after conclusion of the programme of therapy. Even then it was still possible to observe significant improvements. That's almost unheard of for people with dementia! In outpatient care too, relatives have reported that patients were "happier" for as long as three days after therapy.

That sounds fabulous. Has this then become part of the care for people with dementia, in other words has this become standard practice?
D. Muthesius: Unfortunately, it's not covered by health insurance and the small amount of special funding available for people with dementia does not suffice. At the same time, those who work with people with dementia know how important music is. As such, we make the most of fortuitous discoveries

Carers with good social skills are invaluable. Making music together with the residents on a regular basis strengthens the sense of community.

such as relatives who can play the accordion or nurses who can play the guitar. The latter in particular is often beneficial as carers who have a good feeling for music, for example who have no inhibitions about singing, generally also have excellent social skills. Aside from benefitting individual patients, this also helps strengthen community spirit in general.

How should a music therapy room be appointed, for example to be good for group work? What would you ask architects and designers to consider?
D. Muthesius: In my particular field of work, this question is less relevant because we prefer to work with patients where they are, i.e. ideally in their familiar surroundings. It doesn't really matter how nice a music room is … for patients with dementia, any change of scenery is potentially problematic: it is disorientating, which in turn undermines their sense of identity. Moving these people to a music room just creates anxiety.

Put another way: how are rooms designed in which you find you can work particularly well, and what in your experience proves to be problematic?
D. Muthesius: In general, I would say that the success of a music therapy session depends on many other factors, and certainly not on how nice or otherwise the room looks. It is, however, advantageous when people feel comfortable and at home, e.g. if the room is more like a living room, perhaps with furniture that the residents have brought with them. Whether the different cupboards look good in combination is not really relevant; it's about making it homely and familiar. I do remember one occasion, however, where a person with dementia was "amused" by the fact that the three chandeliers in the room came from different stylistic epochs. One should therefore try and avoid too many stereotypes. Sometimes too much decoration can be a problem: tablecloths with nice figurative patterns may be well-meant by the care staff but can be unsettling for people with dementia. What is important

is that the room is bright enough and pleasantly illuminated so that patients feel safe and well.

Homely, cosy and familiar are qualities that architects are often asked to replicate but as terms they are open to interpretation. Do you think that new interiors have been successful in achieving this?
D. Muthesius: How does one define what "cosy" is, let alone design cosiness? More than anything, I think that architecture has to create a sense of normality, i.e. it should avoid confronting residents with an aesthetic environment that is foreign to them and has nothing to do with their earlier life. In a relatively new care home, for example, there is a Japanese garden: it's very, very beautiful, but unfortunately not suitable for people with dementia. The same applies to the corridors facing the interior courtyard that are supposed to provide an outlet for Alzheimer's patients' urge to move around: they are fully glazed on all sides, creating a multiplicity of different views and reflections that ultimately lead to sensory overload. For people who are often unsure of where they are, that does not help their orientation. Fully-glazed walls may be normal for the owners of villas and for architects, but not for our patients.

To come back to the question of the use of music in the therapy of Alzheimer's: how do you think this will develop in future?
D. Muthesius: Leaving aside the problem of funding, current tendencies in the field of education are, I think, particularly alarming. In Berlin, for example, music lessons in schools have been cut back to such a degree that coming generations will have very little in the way of a common stock of music and songs, although they do listen to a lot of music. We are already seeing the first indications of this in our work today. In 30 years' time, people with dementia will not be able to tap into an active repertoire of songs from the past, as they simply did not learn them during their childhood.

The interview was conducted by Christel Kapitzki.

dance and cognition

An interview with Gabriele Brandstetter

Dance is regarded as one of humankind's most primal forms of human expression: is the desire to dance so deeply rooted in us that it can be recalled or animated like other human traits?
G. Brandstetter: It is true that dancing is one of the oldest forms of human expression and manifests itself in many different ways and styles in different cultures around the world. But that does not necessarily mean that it is an innate part of our make-up. Whether people like to dance depends far more on the social, cultural and personal contexts and experiences that have influenced them from an early age. It is hard to say exactly when someone is willing to dance, that is to enjoy dancing, and when they are not; this is something that is better explored together, individually or in small groups.

It has been said that the process of "picking-up" a succession of movements stimulates the brain and that people are able to solve geometric problems, for example, more easily after a dance lesson. Does your experience confirm this, or does this only apply to certain kinds of people?
G. Brandstetter: The ability to "pick up" a sequence of movements stems from one of our fundamental skills as human beings, namely the ability to imitate, to copy, which Aristotle already identified as being a fundamental human characteristic. The act of imitating a sequence of movements is a complex sensorimotoric and cognitive operation: when

someone learns a sequence of steps and associated torso, arm and head movements from an instructor in a dance lesson, the challenge is not purely physical but also cognitive and emotional. This will be more or less successful depending on the person's experience, aptitude and ability to concentrate. Generally speaking, I do think that training, that activating one's rhythmic bodily coordination, moving in space and developing one's proprioception and kinesthetic awareness does have a positive effect on cognitive processes – and this is probably the case regardless of whether the actual dance was performed particularly well or not. What matters is that the process of imitating of a succession of movements, their repetition and memorisation, their variation and perhaps also playful adaptation takes place regularly.

Do you think that this connection can be helpful in the early stages of Alzheimer's?
G. Brandstetter: I have only passing knowledge of the very complex disease of Alzheimer's so I am therefore hesitant about making generalised statements and prognoses. But based on what I've just mentioned about imitating and learning dance sequences, one could conclude that under schooled instruction, dance and movement could be helpful in the early stages of Alzheimer's. But how can they help? Let me briefly outline some of the specific aspects of dance that can be important

within this process: dance constitutes a rhythmic succession of particular patterns of movements (steps, circular movements, changes of direction) which in turn involve spatial orientation; the imitation of a series of steps is a process of transferral, anchored through repetition: and all of these are a fundamental part of the formation and cementation of memory. Some of the oldest treatises on dancing already make special mention of the aspect of "memoria". As the treatment of Alzheimer's aims, among other things, to reinforce memory, to "rediscover" it or to activate new ways of remembering, it seems to me that responsibly instructed dance therapy could be an important and wonderful instrument for practising the memorisation of sequences of movements in a relaxed way in the "here and now". What's important is not the need to do it well but to enjoy the practice of movement itself. We all make mistakes when we practise on our own or together, regardless of how young or old we are.

How should a room be designed or equipped to animate people to dance who have difficulties with spatial awareness?
G. Brandstetter: Designing an ideal space for people to dance in who have difficulties perceiving themselves and the space around them requires that a team of (interior) architects, choreographers/dance therapists and doctors work together.

The design of this façade by architects Böttcher and Dähne in Dresden, Germany, built in 2011, pays respect to the German dancer Gret Palucca.

Gret Palucca (1902–1993) was an internationally known expressionist dancer and dance teacher who lived in Dresden since the 1920s.

A range of conditions needs to be considered, for example that there are no obstructions or tripping hazards. But the space should not simply be "open" – it needs to be structured and usable in a variety of ways. Exactly which ideal constructions are important – such as the ability to regulate light levels – for a room to offer *potential* for dancers with restricted spatial awareness needs to be carefully developed and where necessary perhaps even tested in a model workshop.

Would you say that the spatial interactions that occur when dancing "automatically" promote self-awareness and spatial orientation?

G. Brandstetter: In a recent conversation with a friend of mine who is a choreographer, she spoke of what she called "limited space" while describing an exercise she had set herself. This is a term I find very relevant when considering the way that dance and space can work together in the context of Alzheimer's: the idea of "limited space" as enclosure – as offering clear boundaries and structures that facilitate orientation. At the same time, limited space also implies reduction – a conscious effort to scale down (steps, dimensions or movement) and simplify! This is potentially a most interesting dance, choreographic and architectural exercise if one is willing to consciously take up the challenge and give shape to it. Working under such conditions, carefully and respectfully promoting movement through dance would indeed, I believe, offer the chance to stimulate spatial orientation and the accompanying self-awareness. While this may not happen automatically – much is after all always unpredictable – it is "formative" in the best sense of the word.

It is comparatively rare to see older people dancing – regardless of whether they are handicapped – in our cultural context. That is not the case, though, in Japan. Do you see any indications that things could change here in future?

G. Brandstetter: Yes, these changes are already happening. It is increasingly clear that our cultural context will likewise have to adjust, that the traditional notion of dance as being exclusively youth-oriented – with its concomitant ideals of bodily form and physical capacity – has long been overtaken by developments in the real world. Working together with a young Japanese colleague, Nanako Nakajima, at a conference in 2012 on the "Aging Body in Dance"[1], I discussed these questions with scientists and artists from Eastern and Western cultures. Recently, more and more dancers and choreographers in the West have begun to actively and earnestly address these questions. This issue is, however, relevant not just for dance as an art form. It is important for society as a whole: dancing is a form of movement, of learning, of communication, a way out of loneliness and a means of training body and spirit that is not limited by age. We need to make resources available for such initiatives.

The interview was conducted by Christel Kapitzki.

1   Gabriele Brandstetter and Nanako Nakajima (eds.), *Aging Body in Dance: Seeking Aesthetics and Politics of the Body through the Comparison of Euro-American and Japanese Cultures.* Bielefeld, 2014. www.bewegungsforschung.de/veranst_agingbody2012.html

an interior design concept that appeals to all the senses

Memory panels, boxes and display cases that hold biographical items that pertain to the residents' life histories are an important part of holistic interior design concepts that cater for the specific needs of people affected by dementia. These are typically installed in the hallways and entrance areas of live-in residential facilities to assist orientation and stimulate a sense of identification. As part of therapy, these can be augmented by visual or acoustic stimuli such as birdsong, the sound of a stream gently flowing, or materials that can be touched (such as tree bark), that awake personal memories and invite interaction.

This interior design concept for people with dementia by Mauser Care Furnishing Systems (Germany) was developed in close collaboration with the nursing and care services providers.

midmost – living with dementia

Ann Heylighen, Iris Van Steenwinkel
and Chantal Van Audenhove[1]

Imagine that you leave your house for a walk and hours later have to be traced by your husband because you lost your way. Or that from time to time, you have the impression that past and present intermingle. Or that you feel lonely and fleeting like a dust particle. Such disorientation in space, time, and identity is what Mary — a woman in her forties — is confronted with since she had to learn to live with dementia.[2] Even if she may not be fully aware of being disoriented, the condition can make her feel confused, anxious or even homeless[3] in a world that becomes increasingly complex and incomprehensible to her.

As Mary's relationship with space and time and her sense of self changes, she seems to become less, differently and no longer "automatically" anchored in space. In order to deal with this by reinforcing existing relationships or contesting altered ones, Mary and her husband made changes in their home. Mary started claiming certain spaces in the house and, with the help of her husband and household assistants, (re)organised them in a particular way.

Since she began living with dementia, Mary has claimed particular belongings and spaces in the house for her own. In the kitchen, she has her own cupboard, with her cornflakes, her cup and her glass. It is all hers, always put in the same place, and no one should touch it. At the dining table, she has a chair reserved for her and likewise in the sitting area, her special armchair, with her blankets, her basket, her coffee table, her books, her drinks and her candy. She cannot stand that someone else – not even her husband – sits in her chair or eats her candy without asking, although she knows this might be ridiculous.

The places in the house that Mary claims for her own are organised in such a way that they make it easier for her to mediate space – easier in terms of physical and cognitive effort. She created as it were little worlds for herself, which are narrow enough to provide a protective environment and offer personal places where she has her belongings ready-to-hand.[4] A case in point is her armchair in the living room with her blankets, pillows, books, candy etc. close to her. In the evening Mary and her husband close the curtains, put up the shutters and light candles so that this little world's sheltering character is further strengthened. Another example is the small bedroom where Mary often takes a nap in the afternoon. The bed is surrounded by a light and a radio/CD player she can turn on or off with a single switch; a bottle of water and a cup for her medication; some books and a remote TV control; a headset, CDs, teddy bears and extra pillows – all things she uses on a daily basis.

Looking onto increasingly flat perspectives. Werner Heldt: "Stillleben vor Häusern" (Still life in front of buildings), 1951

The objects at the side of the armchair or the bed are ready-to-hand for Mary both physically and cognitively. Physically, they are ready-to-hand because they are easily accessible: she just has to stretch her arm to grab what she wants while seated in her chair or lying in her bed. Cognitively, they are ready-to-hand first, because they are familiar to her: she uses them daily; second, because they are put in the right place, ordered where they belong; and third, because they have a certain direction and distance in relation to Mary, when seated in the armchair or lying in the bed.

As a result, Mary does not need to search too much. She may even find them with her eyes closed. This "ready-to-hand-ness" seems key to her little worlds: having things close to her armchair, next to her bed or inside her kitchen cupboard makes it easier for Mary, especially when she is not feeling well. This "making-it-easy-on-herself" is a necessary and inventive way for Mary to manage her environment.

The fact that people like Mary who are living with dementia are increasingly disorientated in space, time and identity may not be a surprise, as these dimensions are strongly interrelated.[5] For all three, home constitutes a special point of reference, an anchor point in our life world. "In an ideal sense," the geographer Yi-Fu Tuan writes, "home lies at the center of one's life, and center [...] connotes *origin* and *beginning*."[6] Home offers us a protective place from which we explore the outside world.[7] It is a particularly meaningful place that shapes and reflects our identity.[8] Through furnishing, decorating and tidying up we make the house our own.

Ownership may be understood in a legal sense, yet Mary's example makes clear that it may also refer to "being in control",[9] for instance, over who is allowed to sit where or to eat candy. "Identification is: to own," John Habraken writes, "If you cannot identify yourself [with the house], then you do not dwell, then you lodge."[10] Including identity as a dimension of orientation thus implies that orientation is considered not merely a matter of way-finding, i.e. knowing how to get from one location to another, and relates to questions like: can I be myself here? Can I find a place for my own? Do I feel at home in this place?[11]

While time, space and identity are strongly interrelated for all of us, the existence of this interrelatedness is highlighted because and when it is being contested by dementia. People like Mary might thus help us understand how our orientation in time, space and identity functions, and becomes dysfunctional respectively, and how home features as an anchor point. By claiming certain spaces and belongings in the house, it is as if Mary attempts to maintain or restore connections with her environment, as if she engages consciously in "home-making", investing extra effort in becoming "present", "related" and "part of".[12]

All too often, dementia is assumed to obliterate people's ability to share their experiences with others.[13] In making changes in her house, however, Mary makes her experiences explicit not only as verbal account, but also in the (re-)organisation of the little worlds she creates. Because of her altered relationship with space, time and her sense of self, the little worlds she creates make observable how she tries to maintain as many connections as possible to the house she had made her own before living with dementia, and what adaptations she makes in order to feel comfortable. In living with dementia, Mary thus helps us gain a nuanced understanding of how we may design living environments where people (with and without dementia) may feel at home, or at least may feel at ease, by reducing their feelings of confusion and anxiety.

1   This essay is based on research funded by the European Research Council under the European Community's 7th Framework Programme (FP7/2007–2013)/ERC grant agreement n°201673 and the Research Fund KU Leuven (OT/12/051). Special thanks go to Mary for introducing us into her "little worlds".

2   After seeing Mary in a talk show on TV, we invited her to participate in our research. The second author visited her three times to conduct semi-structured interviews. Mary showed her round the house and explained how she and her husband furnished it and why.

3   J. Frank, "Semiotic Use of the Word 'Home' Among People with Alzheimer's Disease", in: G. D. Rowles and H. Chaudhury (eds.), Home and Identity in Late Life. New York 2005, pp. 171–196.

4   O. F. Bollnow, Human space. London 2011.

5   E. T. Hall, The Hidden Dimension, Garden City. New York 1969; Bollnow, op. cit.; C. Norberg-Schulz, Existence, Space and Architecture. London 1971; J. Piaget, The Child's Conception of Time. London 1969.

6   Y.-F. Tuan, Space and Place. The Perspective of Experience. London 1977, p. 127 (emphasis by the authors).

7   Bollnow, op.cit.

8   Tuan, op.cit.; A. Madanipour, Public and Private Spaces of the City. London 2003; S. Chapman, "A 'new materialist' lens on aging well. Special things in later life", in: Journal of Aging Studies 20 (2006), 3, pp. 207–216; I. Van Steenwinkel et al., "Home in later life. A framework of the architecture of home environments", in: Home Cultures 9 (2012), 2, pp. 195–218.

9   Madanipour, op.cit., p. 63.

10 J. Habraken, "De mens in de stad van de mens". Alphen a/d Rijn 1969, cited in H. Heynen et al., Dat is architectuur. Rotterdam 2004, p. 431 (translation by the authors).

11 I. Van Steenwinkel et al., "Spatial Clues for Orientation", in: P. Langdon et al. (eds.), Designing Inclusive Systems. London 2012, pp. 227–236.

12 K. Zingmark, Experiences related to home in people with Alzheimer's Disease, Umeå University Medical Dissertation, 2000.

13 V. Cotrell and R. Schulz, "The perspective of the patient with Alzheimer's disease", in: The Gerontologist 33 (1993), 2, pp. 205–211.

Everyday habits artistically transformed in designs for new ways of leading one's life. Andrea Zittel: "A-Z Comfort Units", 2010

house

and

courtyard

The perforated nested shells of House N patio garden house in Oita, Japan, built by Sou Fujimoto in 2008 for his parents-in-law

layers of living

On the anatomy of the house

Insa Lüdtke

To experience something
I step out into the hall:
I open the door to the hall
and in the hall close the door to my room
and in the hall open the door to my room
and in my room close the door to the hall:
by
stepping out into the hall
to experience something
I experienced
for the time of stepping out
that I stepped out into the hall.

Peter Handke[1]

Entering and exiting

A door both divides and connects spaces. It facilitates these two opposing possibilities but also unites them. Whether entering or exiting – what we are essentially experiencing is an interconnected, oscillating movement: only what can be opened can also be closed. To leave one room and enter the next is therefore not merely a simple gesture of movement in one direction. It is also a dynamic act of physical articulation in space and as such also an existential human experience.

The door symbolises the entire spectrum of basic human needs – the need for safety and security as well as for autonomy and freedom. As an architectonic element, it denotes the availability of spatial options and offers people the freedom to decide and to act according to their needs.

A door makes a wall permeable. It changes a contained space into a dynamic boundary in which we live. It can provide a sense of sanctuary as well as choice and independence, and in conjunction with fellow humans it presents opportunities for dialogue and interaction. Like the door, a house can also be considered a dialectic boundary in which we live. People with dementia are known to feel restless and to want "to go home". But in this case home does not necessarily mean a house in the sense of a building: rather, home is an emotional place where they can be *themselves*, where they can feel *at home* and at one with themselves. Here they feel safe, and this is the basis from which they can venture out into the world.[2]

Inside and outside

In German, the verb *wohnen* – to abide, to dwell – originates from the old Germanic word *wunian*, which broadly speaking means "to be at peace" – to be free from harm and danger, to be safeguarded in the sense of being able to remain in peace.[3] The verb *wohnen* is also related to "Gewohnheiten", to "habit" and the process of "growing accustomed to". The body grows accustomed to a space by internalising its actions within it. A series of actions, undertaken regularly, becomes a ritual, a habit. They too are comforting. In a new home it is not the rooms themselves that create familiarity, but the new rituals we develop as we get used to them, as we *inhabit* them.[4] With each phase of life, our living requirements – space, number of rooms and their disposition – may change, but what does not change is our basic need for sanctuary and autonomy.

When elaborating a suitable matrix for a house for people with dementia, it seems that, regardless of cultural and historical context, the primary requirements are of a universal nature. A living environment needs to provide a structure that is both as stable and as flexible as possible, that conveys a sense of constancy while accommodating diverse needs and being adaptable – parameters that seem to apply for all human beings.

The typology of the Roman courtyard house was one of the first to establish a complementary connection between indoors and outdoors. It groups the living spaces around an internal courtyard, and makes the atrium, the outdoor space, part of the interior. The inversion of the typical constellation of indoors and outdoors, results in a spatial continuum of the two. This contradictory desire for intimacy on the one hand and a connection to the outdoors on the other is still anchored deep in our subconscious, as shown in a study undertaken by the ifss in Potsdam (Institut für Soziale Stadtentwicklung e.V.) in 2003. The study, undertaken on behalf of German housing and tenants's associations, interviewed 1600 people in eight cities in Germany about their living preferences and showed them various different types of houses and floor plans. By far the most popular living typology was the courtyard house with garden.

Shifting layers
A clear but also non-deterministic approach to handling spatial configurations can be seen in traditional Japanese houses: Japanese townhouses are commonly oriented towards the street and have façades that can often have up to four separate layers of sliding screens that can be totally closed or opened. Alongside the *shoji*, sliding screens made of translucent paper or glass, there are the *amado*, heavy wooden doors that protect against the rain. Similarly the zone directly in front of the house does not have one set purpose. It can be both pathway, and thus part of the street or also be used as a workshop or shop (*machi-ya*), making it part of the house.

The *engawa* is also neither fully an indoor space nor an outdoor space but a transitional space that marks the zone between the house and the outdoors. It has the same floor level as the indoor spaces, which are laid out with *tatami* mats made of rice straw, but is open to the garden outside. It is roofed over, but unlike a veranda it has no balustrade. Here too, *shoji* can be used to temporarily close it off from the interior. The roofed over zone protects the inner sliding screens from driving rain and the interiors from overheating in summer. Although the *engawa* lies outside the interior, people do not wear outdoor shoes on it as it is not considered as being an outdoor space. To properly venture outside, one must consciously step out onto a large stone that serves as a step into the garden.[5] The duality of the *engawa* is also evident in its function: in summer it serves as a shaded outdoor corridor and anteroom-like space while in winter it allows one to enjoy the warmth of the sun.

Spatial zones that are open for different uses can simultaneously provide a sense of security as well as self-determination. This simultaneity is especially important for people with dementia, as they need to feel safe but not confined.

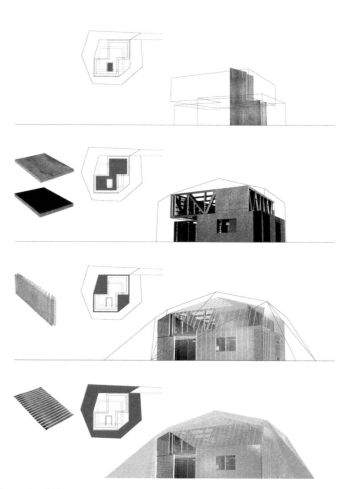

The walls of the Wall House consist of four layers: a reinforced concrete core, timber frame elements, highly-insulated polycarbonate panels and textile membranes.

The radial arrangement of the Wall House in Santiago de Chile, completed in 2007, was designed by FAR Frohn & Rojas as a retirement home.

Safety and security we associate with being *inside* where it is warm, secluded, enclosed and dark. The further out we go, the brighter, lighter and airier it gets. The Wall House is conceived as a retirement home and employs a system of successive layers akin to that of an onion, which despite its schematic structure, has been realised with considerable purpose. The house is radial in structure with walls that consist of four separate layers, each of which has their own quality in terms of function, construction, surface, atmosphere and climate.

The inner layer, the most intimate zone, consists of a reinforced concrete core that contains the wet rooms. From here, one progresses to the second layer which consists of timber elements that can be opened and closed to connect or separate spaces. This also contains storage space. The third layer is made of highly insulated polycarbonate panels. This defines the outer skin of the building and is completely glazed on two sides. Room-height sliding doors make it possible to completely open this layer to the outdoors. The fourth and outermost layer spans the entire house like a tent. It consists of two separate woven membranes that can be used to respond to the ambient climatic conditions. One of the membranes reflects sunlight to prevent overheating and the other serves as an insect screen. The distance between the polycarbonate shell and tent varies from between half a metre and four metres, depending on the rooms within.

Meaning and emotion

Dwelling means on the one hand to make oneself at home and on the other to realign oneself anew to meet changing situations in life, i.e. to find the best place to sleep, to eat, to play, to work, to pack things away, as well as to assess its dimensions, weigh up its atmosphere and to shape it. This is far more than merely a matter of organisation: it is about taking possession of one's territory, about investing it with one's own personality, about becoming one with it.

It is through this that we invest our surroundings with meaning and sensations that go beyond the mere functional aspect of its furnishings. As we enrich our environment with things, our identity accumulates in the space we live in. These extracts of the life we live become part of our repository of memories and serve as points of reference that confirm our image of ourselves. Collecting things and displaying one's treasured possessions are needs that are rooted deep within us, that strengthen our sense of identity and give comfort. Things can recall personal histories, evoke associations and represent the atmospheric and emotional cornerstones of a layer that contributes to our identity.

Rooms without walls. Only the ceiling defines the spaces within the interior of the House Asama in Karuizawa, Japan. Atelier Bow-Wow, 2000

A phenomenological conception of space has also made inroads into the field of materials research, through the vision of our built environment as a dynamic place of exchange and communication. If we see dwelling as an ongoing dynamic process, there is no reason why a room cannot be transformed from a static object into a dynamic subject. Researchers are already investigating how architecture can be conceived, designed and realised as a responsive system, that interacts with its environment and, through the use of hybrid materials and interactive textiles, can externalise one's inner experiences and express them through the architecture.[6] Composite materials are being developed that exhibit the typical characteristics of a material, for example the haptic qualities of knitted material, but also have digitally controllable properties. Using integrated sensors and actuators, the materials can perceive their environment and respond to it.

As part of the research project "Poetic Textiles for Smart Homes", the British designer Carole Collet combined new technologies with traditional techniques. Instead of being purely functional or decorative, or "fixed in time", as Collet says, poetic textiles should create a new quality, either by playing with unexpected materials or by establishing another layer of interaction that "reveals" our domestic rituals.[7]

Compact living

Over the course of a lifetime, whether as a consequence of old age or otherwise, people must learn to come to terms with and to compensate for physical and mental impairments. For us to be able to maintain our quality of life and our mobility, the house and also the environment in which we live must be able to accommodate and respond to these changes. In addition to layering and compressing, a reduction of radius and form can also be a further means of enabling us to lead independent lives in old age or when living with dementia.

A single room, for example, can accommodate an entire way of life: in House Asama (2000) the zoning of the floor plan – kitchen and dining area, living area, work zone, sleeping area and bathroom – is delineated on the underside of the roof construction. Although there are no walls, the shape of the roof – its breadth, depth, roof incline – as well as the visual connection to the world outside define different parts of the space. As the sun travels around the sky during the day, the sunlight changes the atmosphere of the spaces: by the evening, most of the roof is in shade and only the west side glows orange with the light of the descending sun as it shines through the skylight.

In 1951, Le Corbusier designed his minimal house, Le Cabanon, in the form of a 3.66 × 3.66 metre hut. Some 60 years later, the Japanese architect Sou Fujimoto developed a design for the Final Wooden House (2008), a kind of miniaturised matrix for living made of solid blocks of timber. Its intention is to gauge the possibilities of compact living through an extreme degree of abstraction. The house resembles a sculpture made of projecting and receding steps that can be used alternately as stairs, a seat, a bed, table or shelves. The previously separate typologies of living are brought together here in a smart but also sensual cave in which the walls, floor and ceiling are part of the same structure. Sou Fujimoto explains that, "although only a few square metres in size, the house offers people new possibilities as they can move around in it in ways they are not used to." For him, buildings are interactive, haptic playing fields. The way one lives together in such spaces requires more interaction than in expansive apartments with clearly separated areas. The idea and purpose of such micro-architecture is not as an antithesis or rejection of civilisation. Rather it is a tool that holds up a mirror to the rituals of daily life that we take for granted.[8]

The human habitat consists of many diverse aspects, all of which are equally subject to changing conditions, and which must be reappraised from time to time, and especially in old age: its spatial articulation, its enclosure and delineation, its sensory qualities, materials, haptic qualities, forms, measurements and proportions.[9] The consequence does not have to be cramped conditions and loss of possibilities. Strategies such as layering, and making things and places open for multiple uses can condense a lot into a small space and make it possible to create spaces not just of great intensity but also of breadth and freedom. Not only in everyday life is it a pleasant relief to only have to take care of a small space. When, in the manner of self-similarity[10], the neighbourhood relates to the city in the same way that the house does to the neighbourhood and the room to the house, where we choose to live our lives will always remain familiar – and we will be able to live in it as we are used to.

 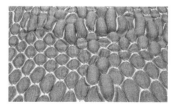

"Listener", developed in 2010 by Mette Ramsgard Thomsen is a textile, robotic membrane that responds to touch and movement.

The Final Wooden House by Sou Fujimoto is a stacked assembly of solid timber beams re-erected in southern Japan in 2008.

1 P. Handke, "Zeitmaße, Zeiträume, Ortszeiten", in: *Die Innenwelt der Außenwelt der Innenwelt.* Frankfurt am Main 1969. To the best of our knowledge, this poem has not been translated into English. The translation provided here is by J. Reisenberger.

2 G. Bachelard, *The Poetics of Space.* New York 1964.

3 M. Heidegger, "Building Dwelling Thinking", in: *Poetry, Language, Thought*, translated by A. Hofstadter. New York 1971.

4 W. Schmid, *Mit sich selbst befreundet sein. Von der Lebenskunst im Umgang mit sich selbst.* Frankfurt am Main 2004.

5 H. Engel, *Measure and Construction of the Japanese House.* Rutland and Tokyo 1985.

6 F. Eidner and N. Heinich, "Technikpoesie, Technologie, Design und Emotion", in: *Baunetzwoche #185 Special*, 2010.

7 *Ibid.*

8 N. Kietzmann, "Wohnen als Werkzeug", in: *Designlines* 16 July 2013, www.baunetz.de.

9 S. Baumers, A. Heylighen and I. Van Steenwinkel, "Home in later life. A framework for the architecture of home environments", in: *Home Cultures*, 9 (2012), 2, p. 195–217.

10 In the strict sense of the word, self-similarity is the property of things, bodies, quantities or geometric objects to exhibit similar or identical properties at different degrees of magnification or scales of dimension. This property is studied in fractal geometry, as fractals (Latin *frāctus* meaning "broken") exhibit a high and sometimes exact degree of self-similarity. The term is also used in a broader sense in philosophy and the social and natural sciences to describe structures that contain recurring patterns of sub-structures. (source: www.wikipedia.org)

The residents may use the interior as they please. A replica of the Final Wooden House was shown at the Kunsthalle Bielefeld, Germany, as an outpost of the documenta 2012.

EXCURSUS

living in
the kitchen

Open kitchen and living areas play a key
role in the care of people with dementia as
a centre of daily life. They enable the residents to take an active part in everyday life
and convey a sense of normality – concepts
that are integral to modern care concepts
used around the world. The kitchen is the
focus of daily routines and engages all the
senses: it is not only a place for cooking
and eating, but a place for cleaning, iron-
ing, chatting, laughing and discussing ... in
short, it is the focus of communal life.

Open kitchen and living areas that afford
a good view of the adjacent corridors as
well as the cooking island, and that adjoin
the pantry, utility room and bathroom also
help care staff go about their diverse everyday tasks while remaining in close contact
with the residents.

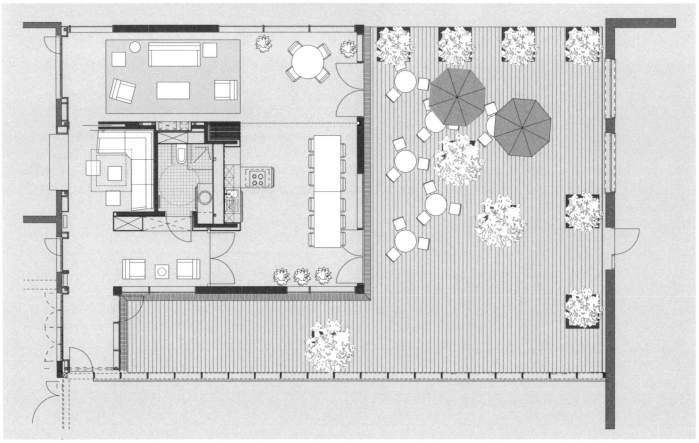

typological grids

Sustaining the familiar through the full cycle of life

Susan Black

Let's imagine – *it is 2030*; a parent no longer suffers from Alzheimer's as stem cells have virtually eliminated neurodegenerative diseases. At the same time, a child is born; genome sequencing is done immediately, a genetic profile prepared and a road map for health predictors firmly established. Genetic wiring towards obesity, a predictor of various chronic ailments including diabetes and dementia, may be reversed – curtailing what is anticipated to be a global epidemic. But we are not there yet.

A loved one suffers from Alzheimer's; becoming another statistic in the fastest growing segment of the world's population; still the least catered to in terms of care and optimising environments and in some countries not even recognised for their disease. Numbers are expected to rise worldwide to over 100 million during the next decade – long before stem cells play a part. Further, by 2040 in the U.S. economy alone, the cost of dementia is anticipated to bankrupt this health care system. Largely unconsidered are children whose risk factors, including obesity, are a predictor for Alzheimer's. And women, often caught in the sandwich generation looking after their young and their old – are estimated to become over 2/3 of the Alzheimer's population while being their critical caregivers! Dementia-friendly solutions have been explored for over two

decades and are increasingly able to provide compensating environments. However, while researchers work diligently to thwart, postpone and eventually find a cure, we hone our skills in design with the understanding that for the foreseeable future, long into the ensuing pandemic, we can alleviate merely 1% of the growing challenge.

But we try! Twenty years ago a purpose-built residence for persons with Alzheimer's disease was opened. Named and based upon a facility in Birmingham, England – Woodside Place of Oakmont in Pennsylvania, USA, became a prototype for dozens of facilities throughout North America. Home for 36 residents through mid-moderate stages of Alzheimer's, it has resulted in post-occupancy studies proving that institutional environments were far from appropriate. Woodside became an "archetype" for dementia-friendly design.

Design can facilitate and empower daily rhythms, functions and social interaction such as joy in experiencing garden pathways, bursting with memories while leading back to where you began. Lessening of anxieties and confusion strengthens one's sense of empowerment – initiating a host of opportunities to engage, to be alone, or to prepare three breakfasts in succession regardless of the time of day! A key element at Woodside

Place is the approachable "country" kitchen. Even the staff care station is integrated into the cabinetry to affirm the commitment to a home-like, trusting environment where someone is always ready to lend a hand.

Sometimes, a version of Woodside is integrated into an expansive development for seniors housing, usually located far from cities and towns where one has lived for years. While cost-effective, on lands once used for farms or wildlife, this is beyond urban sprawl. Families lose the ability to reconnect; especially unfortunate when one family member has few memories left which need reinforcing. While the philosophy of "age-in-place" is achieved, social sustainability is at risk. The familiar becomes all too unfamiliar.

Sun City Ginza, in Tokyo, offers yet another typology. Vertical living is the norm for many families all over the world and Japan is no exception. This multi-use high-rise project caters to senior living, dedicating some floors to meet the needs of persons with dementia. The project slips into the urban fabric where the existing culture prevails along the street similar to historic towns and vital urban centres where the new is integrated with the familiar to the benefit of all generations.

At Bridgepoint Health, Toronto, major renovations created two dementia units within a high-rise chronic care hospital. To alleviate frustration from trying to leave the building, we created oversized wooden disks along the wall at handle height.

While staff could use a card swipe at a single "disk", patients were unaware of the actual door, and ended up using this extended wall as an impromptu musical instrument, flicking paper, pencils and other objects from disk to disk in delight! If this simplistic design solution resulted in this level of engagement and joy – imagine what we can do! But we are not there yet.

Throughout the global village there are homeless of every age on the streets, childhood as well as adult obesity, and riots initiated by teenagers who have given up on a life they once dared to expect. Children are future Alzheimer's patients and yet we focus on end stages of the disease creating projects which sustain a select few. Further, current research informs us that the environment has far greater impact, especially on children's health, than genetics or inactivity. We must rethink and conceive of meaningful and flexible solutions to thwart present challenges while anticipating major breakthroughs by 2030.

Perhaps one of the most positive initiatives we can tap into involves a serious mandate towards the creation of healthy neighbourhoods where children will grow up with fewer health risks, and persons living with Alzheimer's can continue as long as possible as important elders in their communities. An environment of familiarity, generated from sensitive urban/exurban typological grids, brings to mind a walkable community within proximities of favourite destinations, guided

The Roskilde Music Festival Pavilion, built in 2013 by Simon Hjermind Jensen, brings together several functions in a village-like complex.

by landmarks along the way. This has been a measure of planning used historically to create neighbourhoods, which become the personalities of the greater city or town.

Children and the person with Alzheimer's disease need to understand their world as vital and secure. An Alzheimer's residence is a microcosm of the civic fabric, and regardless of the intentional but invisible safety nets, it should be vested in the very community the patient understands and will hopefully be able to integrate with on a regular basis. Shouldn't we practice some of the same guidelines in urban planning as we do for dementia-friendly facilities?

Healthy options should be a natural life experience – home cooked meals, healthy lunches, accessible daycare solutions, free sports activities and more. Infrastructure can come from civic mandates for public/private partnerships or other revitalisation incentives which count; further funding can come from savings in the health sector as less expensive ambulatory services combine with other community resources. Architecture will take a profound stance towards achieving the meaningful

and familiar instead of the heroic and merely functional. Perhaps the corner store is part of the solution as sugary snacks are out of sight! Everyday family needs may literally be prescriptions for health, altering the course of pandemics.

But let's dig deeper! We are learning more about mind/body connections. How do we design environments which contribute to life-affirming patterns of thought – knowing that our thoughts can impact what shows up in the body as disease? Can we find measures of authenticity and universality in creating environments which support the whole person in their process of self-care and self-healing?

Alzheimer's facilities should be located in meaningful places, perhaps alongside a whole new initiative for community-based adult and children's daycare projects! Remember that dementia-related facilities might eventually become children's facilities, university congregate living, or other appropriate uses in 2030 – if we imagine the best. Let's use our collective intelligence – let's make it count by investing in the full cycle of life! We could almost be there!

The dementia-friendly design of Woodside Place of Oakmont day care center, by Perkins Eastman Architects, 1991, served as a model for similar projects all over the USA.

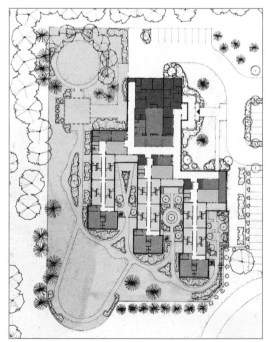

Floor plan and site plan of Woodside Place of Oakmont day care center, USA

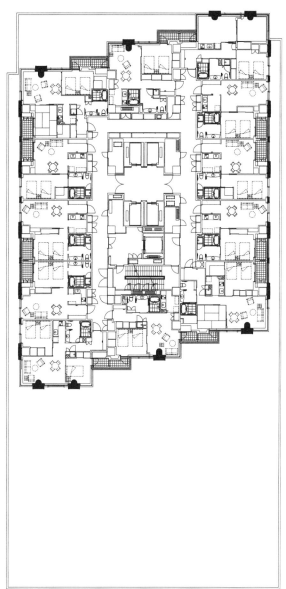

Floor plan of Sun City Ginza East, Tokyo, Japan. Perkins Eastman Architects, 2006

The Sun City Ginza East skyscraper in Tokyo, Japan, was designed specifically as a residence for the elderly and stands high above its 6-storey plinth.

light

Perception and health

David McNair

Role of the brain

Visual perception is a construction by the brain of signals received from the eyes. Six areas within the visual cortex share the work of producing an image. Each has primary but not sole responsibility for different elements of the scene. Briefly, area V1 receives signals from the eye;[1] V2 sends signals to areas V3, V4 and V5 in addition to receiving feedback from them and responding to complex shape characteristics; V3 reacts to lines of specific orientations; V4 is important for colour and orientation, with V4 a crucial communicator; V5 majors in detection of external motion and V6 is strong on cues of self-motion.[2] Given that in people with dementia the communications between these complexes operate under severe stress, with researchers[3] having identified a black flat screen television can be perceived as a hole in the wall, or a Paisley patterned rug as a fish pond, probably even with moving fish, who will judge whether or not people with dementia hallucinate?

In terms of architecture, environments should make use of contrast of tone to aid perception of surfaces and objects, e.g. walls from floors, toilets from floors, food from plates, chairs from floors etc. Confusion and danger of trips can be minimised by ensuring lack of contrast between joins in floor coverings where a step might be perceived when none exists, or drain covers which may be mistaken for holes in external pathways. Objects can deliberately be disguised by lack of tone, e.g. doors for staff in care homes. Bold patterns on surfaces can easily be misinterpreted, and speckled worktops may be set for perpetual cleaning.

Lighting

If insufficient lighting is provided, resulting in low-grade signals from the eye to the brain, how will these connections in the brain function adequately? Most people having dementia are older. Older visual systems are less effective due to increased absorption in the lens and other ocular media, smaller pupil area, a lower number of detection cells in the retina, loss of blood supply to the retina and a reduced number of neurons in the optic nerve and visual cortex.

At the age of 75 years a person requires twice the light that a 45-year-old needs to elicit the same visual response.[4] Commonly, lighting standards are formulated for 45-year-olds. As older people are more susceptible to slips, trips and falls it is advisable not to disadvantage them by providing poor quality lighting.

Sheltered outdoor area. A patio in the Kompetenzzentrum für Menschen mit Demenz, Nuremberg, Germany. Feddersen Architekten, 2006

The principles of good lighting design are:
– to think of reflection and contrast
– to provide good uniformity and a reasonable quantity of light on ceilings and walls
– to avoid sudden changes in light level
– to use lamps with good colour rendition
– to keep glare low

Some people with dementia become confused by inappropriate environments and can think they are trapped in an office or library. Therefore it is recommended that lighting designers use a sufficient number of "domestic" style luminaires[5] in order to help promote recognition of place. Interspersing domestic with discrete commercial can provide the desired appearance together with appropriate energy use.

Circadian rhythm

The suprachiasmatic nuclei (SCN) of the hypothalamus are the body's master clock, initiating biochemical processes important for performance including sleep, heart rate, thermoregulation, alertness and cognition, under the umbrella term circadian rhythm. Since the discovery of the photosensitive retinal ganglion cells (pRGCs) in 2002, much

has been learned about their important role in systemic health. They produce melanopsin, which signals the pineal gland to produce melatonin, the hormone primarily responsible for appropriate function of the SCN.

However, significantly more light is required to trigger the production than is usually found indoors. Insufficient daytime light exposure will result in day-time drowsiness and night-time alertness similar to jetlag. Morning light is particularly important and it should be noted that the peak sensitivity of pRGCs is at 480 nanometres, in the blue part of the visual spectrum. As a consequence exposure to morning day-light is recommended as it has high blue content, preferably outdoors, or indoors where there is good daylight penetration. Conversely, exposure to high levels of blue light in the evening is likely to disrupt circadian rhythms. At the age of 75 years a person requires three times the light that a 45-year-old needs to elicit the same circadian response.[6]

As exposure to light at night can disturb sleep and suppress melatonin production, darkness is preferred. Curtains should block light, and the visual impact of electronic equipment such as monitoring devices, clocks and televisions should be minimised. However, some thought has to be given to lighting the route to the toilet, with a switch by the bed head-board essential and automatic switching on via pressure pad a good option. A constant very low wattage red light in toilets is an option but can be counter-productive in terms of sleep. Options should be controlled by key switch and set up for individual need.

Designers should consider the benefits of maximising day-light while simultaneously using shading devices to minimise unwanted solar heat gain from direct sunlight.

Vitamin D

The positive impact of the hormone vitamin D on bone strength is well known. In addition, deficiency is associated with a range of conditions including colorectal cancer, multiple sclerosis (MS), cardiovascular disease and metabolic syndrome, with researchers unable to determine whether the condi-tions cause the shortfall, or the shortfall the conditions. Perhaps a step towards clarity was taken when in 2010 it was found that vitamin D receptor (VDR) binding sites were significantly over-represented near autoimmune and cancer-associated genes previously identified from genome studies.[7] Although some vitamin D can be obtained from food and sufficient from dietary supplements, a highly efficient source is cutaneous synthesis through short duration exposure of skin to sunlight between spring and autumn equinoxes. However, care should be taken to avoid unprotected exposure of more than a few minutes daily or to midday sun. Although daylight is more important, designers should take into account that easy access to the outdoors will facilitate short exposures to sunlight.

Dementia-friendly lighting

In summary, the primary elements of dementia-friendly lighting are to: [8]
– increase light levels to twice "normal"
– use daylight wherever possible
– expose people to the 24-hour cycle of light and dark
– use sufficient "domestic style" fittings to help
  promote recognition of place

Architectural designs should take account of these elements and may wish to incorporate porches, conservatories, or gazebos to maximise daylight exposure. Daylight penetration into buildings is free and provides an excellent quality of light.

User-oriented therapeutic colour and lighting concept. Fürstlich Fürsten-bergisches Altenpflegeheim, Hüfingen, Germany. GSP architects – Volpp, Amann, Heeg, 2009

1   S. M. Zeki, *A vision of the brain*. Oxford 1993.

2   V. Cardinand and A.T. Smith, "Sensitivity of human visual cortical area V6 to stereoscopic depth gradients associated with self-motion", in: *Journal of Neurophysiology*. Bethedsa 106 (2011), 3, pp. 1240–1249.

3   G. M. M. Jones and W. J. van der Eeerden, "Designing care environments for persons with Alzheimer's disease: visuoperceptual considerations", in: *Reviews in Clinical Gerontology*. Cambridge 18 (2008), 1, pp. 13–37.

4   P. L. Turner and M. A. Mainster, "Circadian photoreception: ageing and the eye's important role in systemic health", in: *British Journal of Ophthalmology*. London 92 (2008), 11, pp. 1439–1444.

5   J. M. Torrington and P. R. Tregenza, "Lighting for people with dementia", in: *Lighting Research and Technology*. London 39 (2007), 1, pp. 81–97.

6   P. L. Turner and M. A. Mainster, op. cit.

7   S. V. Ramagopalan et al., "A ChIP-seq defined genome-wide map of vitamin D receptor binding: Associations with disease and evolution", in: *Genome Research*, 20 (2010).

8   D. G. McNair et al., "Light and lighting design for people with dementia", in: *Dementia Services Development Centre*. Stirling 2013.

A study undertaken between 2007 and 2009 confirmed the positive effect of circadian lighting on the activity and nocturnal agitation of people with dementia.

architectural space, acoustics and dementia

Richard Pollock

When a group of people is asked the simple question "can you think of some sounds you have heard earlier today?", an interesting thing happens. Firstly, they start to focus on the sounds of the moment other than the speaker's voice, and then the challenge comes of trying to remember earlier events of the day and a frantic search for the actual sounds associated with them. This demonstrates a couple of particularly important characteristics of sound and hearing: Firstly, hearing cannot be turned off. Secondly, what we remember hearing is selected by the brain – which cleverly works out what it needs in order for us to understand and function normally in the aural environment.

In urban environments the brain learns to ignore background sounds such as traffic, except, for example, when it is needed to cross a road safely. Similarly, people who live close by the seaside can sleep peacefully at night despite the roar of the waves.

Sound is the sensation produced by a certain range of rapid fluctuations of air pressure affecting the ear mechanism and noise can be described as unwanted or harmful sound. Sound is measured in terms of intensity (decibels or dB) and frequency (Hertz or Hz). Where the ability to hear sound normally can be vitally important to people with dementia, the presence of noise can be a serious nuisance and be actually harmful to their health and well-being. Much research has recently been directed towards the significant health benefits of natural light and a well-lit internal environment, yet little attention has been paid to sound, noise and hearing. We can avert our eyes to avoid glare and close our eyes to sleep but we cannot shut off hearing unless by physically covering or blocking our ears.

We have no ear lids. We are condemned to listen. But this does not mean our ears are always open.
R. Murray Schafer[1]

In designing the acoustic environment it is useful to understand the ageing ear and hearing loss through life. By the age of 70 years over 70 % of people have some kind of hearing loss and over a third have moderate hearing loss. (RNID 2010 – formerly Royal National Institute for Deaf People, now Action on Hearing Loss).

There are three stages involved in hearing and these can be described as detection, resolution and identification:
- Detection is simply noticing that there is a sound.
- Resolution involves establishing where a sound is coming from.
- Identification means being able to understand and name the sound.

Acoustic ceiling in the comfortable restaurant of Multengut senior citizen's residence in Bern, Switzerland.
Burkhalter Sumi Architekten, 2004

The brain strives to interpret these stages from nerve impulses generated by the simple hearing mechanism that passes vibrations from the movement of air molecules on the eardrum via three small, connected bones in the inner ear to the snail-like cochlea. With dementia affecting the brain this process can be severely compromised, which leads to hearing becoming very confused. It is therefore essential that sound is kept as clear as possible and that all unnecessary noise is eliminated.

Hearing structures and articulates the experience and understanding of space.
Juhani Pallasmaa[2]

Are we aware in our day-to-day lives just how much people can be cut off from engaging and being able to communicate simply by being unable to hear and understand what is going on around them? Background noise in a busy café, the end seat at a long, narrow dining table – these can all lead to older people generally and people with dementia especially becoming isolated and withdrawn. Night and day differences need careful consideration. Sounds that are barely audible during daytime background noise can become very much louder and disturbing when everything is quieter at night. People with dementia sometimes experience problems with incongruent sources of sound such as watching ballet on the television whilst a sports commentary is booming out of the radio. There is also the potentially confusing effect when sound is seen to be out of phase with vision as sometimes happens when watching old films where lip movements show that the sound recording is out of timing with the film-track.

To demonstrate the importance of good acoustic conditions, research has shown that a better sound environment contributes positively towards:

– reducing risk of high blood pressure[3]
– preventing an increase in heart rate, respiration rate and blood cholesterol
– improving quality of sleep[4]
– reducing intake of pain medication[5]
– reducing the number of readmissions
– improved well-being among staff and improved perceived performance
– being able to engage and communicate[6]
– improving concentration and coordination

The design challenge for the architect in creating the spaces and internal environment of buildings, is to take into account the five most significant acoustic issues established by the Dementia Services Development Centre at the University of Stirling, UK:

1. Keep noise sources away

When designing a building in its site context and setting, it is vital to pay attention to possible external sources of noise such as traffic (road vehicles, planes, railways, fire & rescue stations etc.) and local neighbourhood facilities that can generate unacceptable levels of noise (factories, sports stadia, cinemas, pubs and clubs etc.).

Spatial layout also needs to take into account internal sources of noise – atria, corridors and circulation spaces, nurse stations, service areas (deliveries, kitchens and laundries etc.) can all generate high levels of noise that make it difficult for people with dementia to function comfortably in the aural environment.

2. Consider structure and construction

Sound and noise in buildings are controlled by absorption, transmission and insulation. In larger spaces, greater areas of absorptive surfaces, such as panels and ceiling tiles, are needed to reduce reverberation to acceptable acoustic levels. Transmission of sound from noisy to quiet rooms can be controlled by means of acoustical separating walls and floating floors. Attention to the detail design and positioning of doors and windows is also essential to prevent the spread of noise from room to room.

3. Consider reverberation time

The size of the space is significant, with larger volumes leading to longer reverberation times. This in turn affects the ability to recall speech. Reverberation times can be modified by the addition or removal of absorptive materials, panels and linings. It is worth noting that when reflected sound reaches a listener more than 0.06 seconds after direct sound, it is heard as an echo.

4. Improve visibility

People who have a hearing impairment rely more on visual clues in their day-to-day life so it is beneficial for them to be provided with good levels of light, both natural and artificial. Smaller spaces tend to make for easier visibility due to enclosing walls, furniture and other people being less distant. The vast majority of us naturally lip read when listening to a person speaking (RNID) and therefore seating should be arranged so that people with dementia can talk face to face, since this arrangement improves hearing and understanding of speech.

5. Use assistive technologies

In a short article it is not possible to cover the contribution various assistive technologies can make to improving the acoustic environment, but we need to remember that the noise created by audible alarms can cause much anxiety and distress for people with dementia who cannot understand what is happening and may tend to panic.

In conclusion, the following quote nicely sums up the importance of the quality of the acoustic environment in architectural space:

Freedom from the harassing effects of noise is one of the finest qualities a building can possess.
Vern Oliver Knudsen and Cyril M. Harris[7]

1   R. M. Schafer, *Open ears. Soundscape: The journal of acoustic ecology.* 4 (2003), 2, pp. 14–18.

2   J. Pallasmaa, *The eyes of the skin: architecture and the senses.* Chichester, 2005, p. 49.

3   V. Blomkvist et al., "Acoustics and psychosocial environment in intensive coronary care. *Occup. Environ. Med.* 62 (2005), pp. 1–8.

4   S. Berg, "Impact of reduced reverberation time on sound-induced arousals during sleep", in: *Sleep* 24 (2001), 3, pp. 289–292.

5   B. B. Minckley, "A study of noise and its relationship to patient discomfort in the recovery room", in: *Nursing Research 17 (1968)*, 3, pp. 247–250.

6   M. McManus, C. McClenaghan and Dementia Services Development Centre (University of Sterling), *Hearing, sound and the acoustic environment for people with dementia.* Stirling, UK, 2010.

7   V. O. Knudsen and C. M. Harris, *Acoustical Designing in Architecture.* Melville 1980, orig. published in 1950.

The diverse wall surfaces in the different residential groups have also an impact on the acoustics. Kompetenzzentrum für Menschen mit Demenz, Nuremberg, Germany. Feddersen Architekten, 2006

norra vram
nursing home

Norra Vram, Sweden

Architects
Marge Arkitekter AB

Client
Partnergruppen AB

Planning
12/2006–12/2007

Construction
04/2008–12/2008

Gross floor area
1,400 m² additional
building extension,
1,000 m²
reconstruction,
total 2,400 m²

Initially the project focused on an analysis of how nursing homes are normally designed and what social effects their design has on the residents, their relatives and the staff. Places were identified where these target groups like to meet and where they find stimuli in their physical surroundings. Alongside places in the home, semi-private and semi-public environments, for example the office, coffee shop, hotel or museum were also considered.

Some of the functions in these areas had the potential to be incorporated into a home for elderly people – functions that not only help stimulate exchange and interaction but also lend the place a sense of home and privacy.

The nursing home in Norra Vram consists of a late 19th century mansion that has been rebuilt and extended. The volumes are designed to aesthetically resemble old Swedish farms, and to complement other houses in the neighbourhood. A couple of mews are placed next to each other and in the spaces between them atrium courtyards are situated. The small green gardens allow residents with medical conditions to enjoy time outdoors by themselves. The volumes are plastered in different colours, picking up the shades in the red brick of the existing mansion.

The first impression of the interior is a spacious and welcoming entrance area. This is a flexible space for gatherings with a reception, a library and a small espresso bar. From here you reach three wards – one for short time staying, one for people with dementia and one for people with physically and mentally impaired ability. All residential rooms are organised adjacent to a communal living room or a green courtyard. In that way, long corridors are minimised on behalf of more stimulating meeting places and focal points. The different wards are connected with each other which make it possible to walk around, as an offer for people with dementia.

A cluster of houses rendered in various shades of brick red

A small outbuilding surrounded by greenery

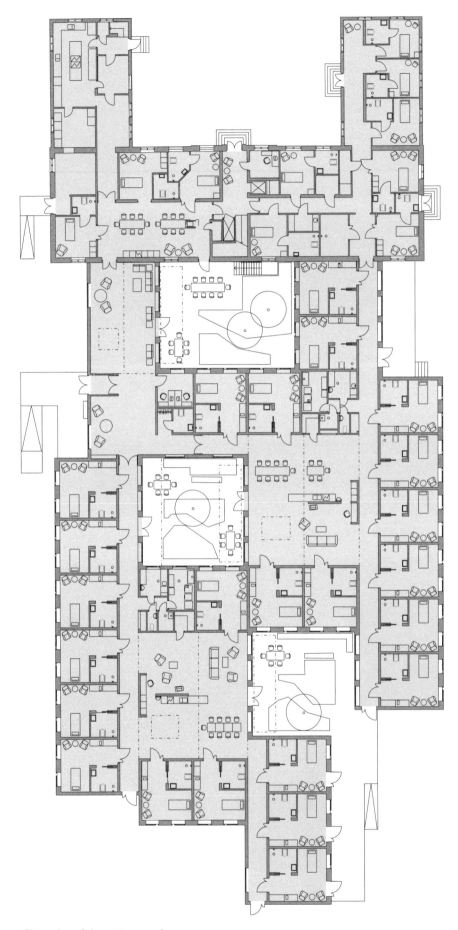

Floor plan of the entire complex

Spacious open areas for socialising

A sheltered private space as a personal retreat

hanna
reemtsma house

Hamburg, Germany

Architects
Dipl.-Ing. Architekt
E. Schneekloth +
Partner

Client
Hanna Reemtsma
House Foundation

Planning
04/2007–08/2011

Construction
06/2008–11/2011

Gross floor area
22,660 m²

After almost forty years as a home for the elderly, a new concept was sought for the Hanna Reemtsma House in Hamburg-Rissen with the aim of creating a contemporary residence for the elderly that addresses both the need for safety and security in old age as well as the wish for a homely environment.

The barrier-free complex is arranged around a service centre containing communal spaces, a restaurant, music room, chapel as well as a room for festivities – all of which are reachable from an underground car park. The service centre is the physical centre of the complex and is framed on one side by five villa-like buildings with a total of 59 two- and three-room apartments, and on the other by a residential care house for three residential groups.

The latter contains a further 41 apartments with open dining and kitchen areas, reception areas and living rooms. The lighting concept and clear arrangement of the floor plan provide safe and easy orientation for the elderly residents. The upmarket design and furnishing of the houses is underlined by the high-quality workmanship of the façades, which are faced with brickwork typical of the region. The buildings' construction and technical installations are also sustainable and ecologically highly modern: using renewable energy from the wood-chip-fired heating plant to the west of the site and solar panels, the complex is energy-efficient and produces its own energy.

The high quality of the interior design is also reflected in the design of the outdoor areas which include a courtyard garden with a south-facing terrace and a large park to the north of the complex. The ensemble of buildings situated amidst mature trees in the middle of a park and alongside a pond evokes associations with a traditional village.

A circular path leads past various attractions, for example a garden of the senses for peaceful contemplation and a boule court for playing games outdoors. The concept of "living in a park" does not end at the edge of the complex: residents can also walk in the Schaakenmoor nature reserve and the game enclosure at Klövensteen, both of which are in the direct vicinity of the complex.

Distinctive and emblematic: view of the service centre

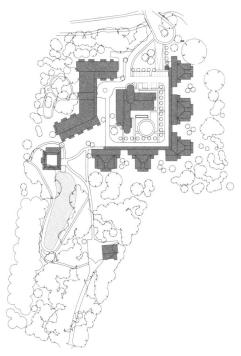

Site plan

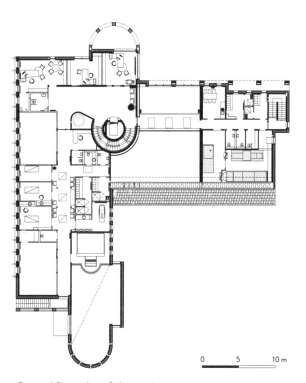

Ground floor plan of the service centre

The residential care house seen from the southeast

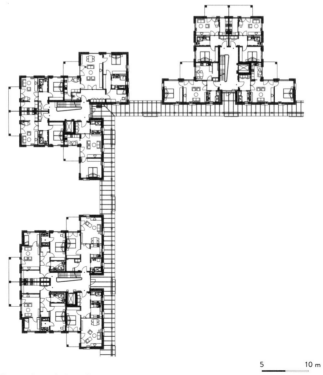

5   10 m

Floor plan of the villas

Covered walkway connecting the villas

gairola house

Gurgaon, Haryana, India

Architects
Anagram Architects

Planning
06/2008–02/2009

Completion
02/2009

Gross floor area
523 m²

In most Indian cities, the typical urban multi-family residence or apartment stack evolves from a semi-detached single family home built on a suburban or peri-urban plot. This evolution occurs with the inevitable agglomeration of such plotted developments, both planned and unplanned, within the urban sprawl. As the city expands, these outlying areas grow increasingly urban, causing the actual city centre to lose significance. As a consequence of the increase in rental values that accompanied the process of urbanisation, many such residences were subdivided into multiple rental units.

As a suburban single family residence, the design of such residences usually follows a typology of the introverted courtyard home that prioritises high levels of privacy and maximisation of covered floor plate. With each plot functioning as a fortified unit of the urban fabric, social rapports with neighbours are restricted to conversations across the shared boundary walls. This typology usually evolves into a two or three decker apartment stack that has similar or identical floor plans with a common access staircase. The role that the staircase, courtyard and setbacks can now play as shared community spaces is frequently neglected.

The idea was to develop this plot purely for the rental market. The design investigates the possibility of creating an extroverted multiple residence apartment stack which exploits the external volumes as shared resources (for light and ventilation) that encourage a vibrant, socially connected, urban lifestyle while still fulfilling the need for privacy and individuality. In order to maximise rental options the stack was conceptualised as a four bedroom duplex, a two bedroom simplex single floor unit and a one bedroom rooftop apartment. This helped to cater to the typical tenant base of nuclear families, young couples and single professionals or students.

As the floor plans of the residences are not identical, the shared courtyard and front setback are no longer simple cuboid volumes but are multi-level sociopetal spaces. The volume of the front setback is split into multiple spatial clusters with increased interconnectivities through a manipulation of enclosed and open volumes. The open staircase combines with a terraced central courtyard to become community space with shared territoriality. Care has been taken to ensure that the increased visual connectivity is restricted to the more public spaces of the apartments. The sheltered sunken court, cantilevered verandah and roof top terrace garden provide each apartment its own private outdoor space. Each apartment has been designed to be a unique home but one that encourages a socially vibrant lifestyle.

Different materials emphasise the contrast between the more open and more closed volumes.

Terraces on the west face of the building

Open courtyard in the building's interior

house of
sense memory

Beth Tauke

Sensory stimuli can trigger memories. A British-led group of neuroscientists recently conducted a study, which revealed that if one of the senses is stimulated to evoke a memory, other memories featuring other senses also are triggered.[1]

Sensory systems

Traditional sensory classification includes vision, hearing, smell, taste and touch. Although many adhere to this system, J.J. Gibson's model, comprised of visual, auditory, taste-smell, basic orienting and haptic systems, is more conducive to design applications. This model considers space as an integral component of sensory perception and warrants a specific definition of space: the sensory fields of experience in which people, objects and events have positions relative to one another. Each system has its own spatial component, and its relation to the other senses is spatial as well. In Gibson's model, the en-vironment is essential to our ability to receive sensory information. Gibson's expanded categorisation of sensory perception provides a foundation upon which design strategies may be employed and evaluated. His system establishes a framework for domestic sensory enhancements such as memory niches, sound gardens and tactile cues. These features can trigger memory, and thus, affect life quality.

The visual system

The visual system has governed the design of the built environment, especially in media-driven cultures. The resulting architecture is visually appealing over all else. Juhani Pallasmaa warns of the potential hazards of this imbalance: "The ocular bias has never been more apparent in the art of architecture than in the past 30 years, as a type of architecture aimed at a striking and memorable visual image has predominated. Instead of an existentially grounded plastic and spatial experience, buildings have turned into image products detached from existential depth and sincerity."[2] If designers fail to recognise the potential for information to be understood through other sensory modes, the predominance of visual stimulation can be problematic.

Despite the overuse of the visual in our culture, its direct application in the home can improve the function and enhance the pleasure of our daily lives. For example, designing a variety of lighting types and levels that are directed towards particular activities can ensure that most people are able to access needed visual information. Alzheimer's patients, in particular, respond positively to full spectrum lighting,[3] and require additional non-glare illumination throughout the home. Dimly lit areas

Rethinking the necessities of life. PARK SERA: "The composition for a chocolate bread 2", PRAC.TICAL.COURSE, 2012

may produce confusing shadows that result in misinterpreting everyday objects.[4] Evenly lit spaces prevent this.[5]

A second application involves differentiating edges using light and color contrast. Stairs with clearly defined treads, rail lighting and automatic sensor lighting at the top and bottom evenly illuminate the most dangerous area in the home. Light and colour play an important role in our physical and psychological senses of well-being. Several studies have demonstrated that a shortage of exposure to daylight or artificial bright light has been linked to the occurrence of mood and behaviour shifts, and that indoor illumination that compensates for seasonal low light levels is beneficial to a sizable portion of the population.[6] Therefore, it is important not only to consider lighting levels, but also the design of timing for illumination.

Colour also affects the way that we take in and process what we see. Although most of us lose some ability to discern subtle contrast between colours as our eyes age, people with Alzheimer's disease experience a greater loss. They have difficulty differentiating colours in the blue-violet spectrum.[7] As a result, it is helpful to establish high contrast conditions that do not require reliance on hue to indicate key information.

For example, grab bars that contrast with walls are preferable. Solid colours, lighter on walls and darker on floors, are less confusing than patterns and prints.

The auditory system

We hear ourselves, others, objects in our environment (the distant train), and we hear space itself (or rather, the way that sound waves respond to surfaces and objects in their path). As such, the auditory system has remarkable potential for spatial definition. Sound can assist in navigation. Although we rarely focus on it, we have the ability to "transform the acoustic attributes of objects and geometries into a useful three-dimensional internal image of an external space ... Listeners who must move around in places without light are likely to ... recognize open doors, nearby walls, and local obstacles."[8]

Often, aural-architects focus on the design of concert halls, theaters and public spaces in which sound is a primary programmatic component. No less important is the design of sound in the home. Home sound design can minimise noise, mark zones of privacy and socialisation, provide alerts and offer spaces that enhance sound pleasures. Techniques for noise-abating design include reducing sound reverberation time, limiting airborne noise, reducing impact noise and minimising background noise.[9] Architects can use sound-absorbing surfaces, such as fabrics, acoustical materials, and vegetation; add sound-absorbing insulation to wall and ceiling cavities and install solid core doors with threshold closures in spaces designed for quietness. Acoustics have the potential to express material, spatial and functional characteristics. In our homes, this can indicate programme. For example, bathroom surfaces often are made of porcelain and tiles to avoid water absorption. The splashing of water on the tile floor and click of the toothbrush on the sink identify the bathroom as a place of cleansing. These sounds are familiar and to the person with Alzheimer's disease, this familiarity provides grounding.

Smoke alarms, stove timers and dryer alerts most often are sound-based. We rely on these systems to keep our homes operating safely and efficiently. Of primary importance is the sound range of these devices. Although we can generally hear frequencies between 20 Hz and 20,000 Hz, this range varies significantly with age, occupational hearing damage and gender. The human ear is most sensitive to frequencies around 1,000–3,500 Hz.[10] All warning systems should cover this range. Sound-based alarms should offer other sensory prompts such as light and/or motion. The difficulty with alarm design is that those with dementia often are startled by these alerts; instead of responding appropriately, they can freeze or become agitated. Further testing in this area is necessary for evidence-based recommendations.

Sound experts Blesser and Salter remind us that "just as visual embellishments can make a space aesthetically pleasing to the eye, so aural embellishments can do so for the ear, by adding aural richness to the space."[11] When considering the aural characteristics of our homes, we might move beyond sound reduction, isolation and absorption and into positive acoustic design as well.[12] When used appropriately, sounds and music can shift mood, manage stress-induced agitation, stimulate positive interactions, facilitate cognitive function and co-ordinate motor movements. Responses to sound are influenced by the motor centre of the brain that responds directly to auditory rhythmic cues. When developing an aural palette for a home, designers might not only consider the physical/spatial support system to ensure sound quality, but also consult with the occupants to ensure choices and levels that are both stimulating and enjoyable.

The taste-smell system

According to Gibson, taste and smell are an interdependent system, which stimulates our desire to eat and warns us of various dangers.[13] This system affects our preferences and aversions and, as such, influences how we act and feel. Strong correlations have been found between taste-smell

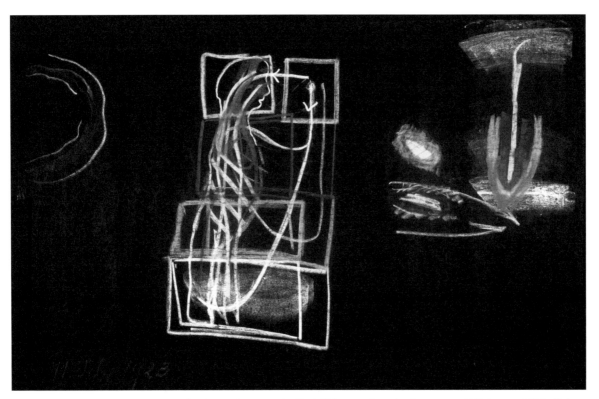

"The Invisible Human Being In Us". Blackboard drawing by Rudolf Steiner from his lecture on 11 February 1923, Colour Plate 3, Volume XII of "Wandtafelzeichnungen zum Vortragswerk" (The Blackboard Drawings)

and attention, reaction times, mood and emotional state.[14] Taste-smell can stimulate the memorisation of concepts or experiences. Odors are well known for their high influence as contextual retrieval cues not only for autobiographic memories, but also for various other types of memory, including visuospatial memories.[15] Designers often neglect taste-smell as a part of spatial definition. The geographer Yi-Fu Tuan reminds us, that "odors lend character to objects and places, making them distinctive, easier to identify and remember".[16] Each home has an individual scent. Various materials, such as wood, characterise space with their odors. Others, such as textiles, absorb the odors of inhabitation. Occupants' actions can determine the scent of each room, which, in turn, suggest what behaviours take place in these spaces. The taste-smell system can be used as a home design element. Materials can identify various spaces with specific scents. For instance, rooms might be surfaced with odiferous materials such sandalwood, or odor reflecting materials such as porcelain or glass. Olfaction can affect behaviour and mood.[17] Introduction of scent way to influence performance has been practiced in industry for some time. Peppermint and citrus have been introduced into the air handling systems of factories to increase worker productivity.[18] The introduction of scent into various domestic spaces in our homes can affect us as well. For example, the smell of baking bread might stimulate our appetites. Scents such as chamomile, known to promote relaxation, might be introduced into bedrooms. Offices might contain materials such as cypress that increase alertness. To be effective in concert, however, the design of taste-smell systems in the home requires restraint, balance and precision.

Deficits in taste-smell detection and discrimination are among the earliest symptoms of Alzheimer's disease. The changes taking place in the olfactory system may be similar to those in other regions of the brain but appear more rapidly.[19] Despite the early onset, it is rare that individuals completely lose this sense. Moreover, taste-smell senses are the most direct and have the power to awaken memories. Therefore, after investigation about which taste-smell sensations are positive for residents, consider adding memory evoking olfactory features.

More essential is the flexibility of taste-smell design elements to accommodate those with airborne sensitivities and olfactory-gustatory disorders. For example, air filtration systems give occupants control of air flow/purification and in turn, the type and level of scent in living spaces. In addition, dangers that are detected by smell, such as gas leaks, need supplemental warning systems that engage other senses. Taste-smell impairments can cause a loss of interest in food. Conductors that control food smells can address issues that accompany meal preparation. The inclusive design of the taste-smell system in the home is challenging because of its pervading nature. Designers might focus on innovations that offer adaptability and contain the infusion of taste-smell in ways that allow us to enjoy its many benefits.

The basic orienting system
The basic orienting system allows us to understand our position in space; it establishes a sense of up/down and left/right, which in turn, sets up our posture and balance. Gibson specifies that along with the basic orienting system "goes a basic type of perception on which other perceptions depend, that is, the detection of the stable permanent framework of the environment ... a dim, underlying and ceaseless awareness of what is permanent in the world".[20] This system establishes within us a sense of gravity and our supporting surface; the distinction between sky above and earth/water below, which helps to identify the horizon, the location of events/objects in the environment, oriented locomotion and geographic orientation.

The basic orienting system coupled with the haptic system, according to Gibson, is predominantly responsible for our three-dimensional experience of space. Through this sense we balance equilibrium of posture with the force of gravity. We subconsciously define the edges and contours of solids and reveal options for movement. The built environment becomes a control, while bodies forever change position, resulting in the experience of new spatial arrangements. Through this process, we continuously add to our understanding of location.

The basic orienting system in the home involves the creation of reference points for occupants so that they can understand their spaces. For example the house entrance is a key marker that should be detectable by all. Entrance marking might include: a brightly coloured door, an overhang etc. Also important is the reciprocal relationship between inside and outside: for example windows might be placed to mark the horizon line or position changes of the sun. Air passages might be situated to let the sounds of front and back to reference the way the house is sited. Basic orientation instills a sense of stability, and requires multi-sensory strategies. Our basic orienting system is closely tied to memory. Primary cognitive mappings usually include space orientation in our homes. For those with fading memories, moving to a new house with a different spatial organisation can be confusing. In these situations designers might use more intuitive floor plans.

The haptic system
The haptic system is considered as the "mother of our senses". Skin is our most direct link to the world. We feel spaces with

Entrance niches and built-in residents' boards mark where the residents live and reinforce their sense of identification. Kompetenzzentrum für Menschen mit Demenz, Nuremberg, Germany. Feddersen Architekten, 2006

our haptic system. Despite this, the power of touch, pressure and temperature often are overlooked by designers. As we age, our senses begin to lose precision. Consequently, we rely more on haptic cues because they are the most local. Tactile stimulation has a positive effect on individuals with Alzheimer's disease. A recent study in the Netherlands revealed that patients who were given tactile stimulation received short-term benefits; they felt less depressed and anxious, more well tempered and alert. Their personal environmental orientation improved. They were more interested in social contacts. They participated more in activities of daily living.[21] Hapticity becomes increasingly important as the disease progresses. Stroking a pet or touching soft fabric can comfort a person whose other senses have diminished.

Haptically sensitive strategies in residential architecture can bypass other sensory modalities. The feel of certain materials indicates specific behaviours. The bedroom for instance, often consists of softer, warmer materials, indicating a place of rest. In contrast, the kitchen surfaces areas tend to be harder, evoking activities such as food preparation and clean up. The environmental psychologist Edward T. Hall recognises the importance of this, but also notes that the "texture of surfaces on and within buildings seldom reflects conscious decisions; thus our ... environment provides few opportunities to "build a kinesthetic repertoire of spatial experiences".[22] Inclusive architectural practices promote attention to the haptic system, and nowhere is this more meaningful than in the home. Rethinking the domestic environment to elevate its tactile qualities sets up support for a wider range of people and provides richer information about their living environment. For example changes in floor textures can identify various spaces, establishing a subtle yet effective map of the home. Floor temperatures can be regulated to provide seasonal balance. Handrails can be textured to indicate step rhythms, beginnings and endings. Surfaces that come in contact with the human body can be made safer: tub/shower floors might contain surfaces to prevent slipping. Faucet handles can indicate safe levels of hot and cold. Exploring the potential of the haptic system within the home allows us to "get in touch" with our bodies. In this way, the experience of home might become one of rediscovering the importance of grounding and extending ourselves through touch.

Interdependent and inclusive sensory systems
Experiencing architecture involves all the senses. However, "only a few studies have explored the way in which multisensory architecture influences the inhabitants of a space".[23] Inclusive design is primary among the approaches most conducive to investigate sensory experience in architecture. Its reach should include designing for those with Alzheimer's disease. The challenge for designers is to develop convincing proposals that not only enrich conventional concepts of space, but also open choices for those with memory loss.

The home is the place to start this challenge. Homes, the spatial records of our identity, are places where we should be able to be our most vulnerable selves. The incorporation of multi-sensory design strategies that reinforce our experiences, help us to more fully engage our homes; even as memories fade, we are able to enjoy the spaces of our daily lives.

Thin rubber strips sandwiched between ash-wood battens can be used to wipe off water after showering and can also be used for a back massage.

Haptic bathroom in the La Marche Residence in Derby, New York, USA

1 M. Hopkin, "Link Proved Between Senses and Memory", in: *Nature: International Weekly Journal of Science*, May 31, 2004. www.nature.com/news/1998/040524/full/news040524-12.html (March 2012).

2 J. Pallasmaa, *The Eyes of the Skin. Architecture and the Senses.* Chichester, Sussex 2005, p. 30.

3 M. Davis, "Good Day Sunshine", in: *Perspectives: Research and Creative Activity,* University of Illinois at Carbondale, Fall 2005, http://perspect.siu.edu/05_fall/alzheimers.html, (February 6, 2013).

4 National Institute on Aging, *Home Safety for People with Alzheimer's Disease,* U.S. Department of Health and Human Services, NIH Publication no. 02-5179, August 2010.

5 The LIFEhouse™ is located at Newport Cove, New American Homes' award-winning waterfront community on Bluff Lake in Antioch, Illinois. The LIFEhouse™ integrates universally designed features into the home such as no-step entrances, wide doorways and passageways, accessible bathrooms with no-step showers and roll-under sinks, accessible kitchen and laundry, an elevator to the lower level, auditory and visual safety features, built-in communication system, numerous lighting levels in each room, memory niches for keys and other items near every entrance, easy-opening windows and doors and energy-saving features. www.newport-cove.com/ (December 1, 2012).

6 S. Grimaldi et al., "Indoors illumination and seasonal changes in mood and behavior are associated with the health-related quality of life", in: *Health Quality of Life Outcomes* 56 (2008). Published online August 1, 2008. www.pubmedcentral.nih.gov/articlerender.fcgi?artid=2527305, (February 25, 2013).

7 "The Alzheimer's Eye Sees Things Differently", in: *The Eldercare Team.* www.eldercareteam.com/public/677.cfm (January 11, 2013).

8 B. Blesser and L.-R. Salter, *Spaces Speak, Are You Listening? Experiencing Aural Architecture.* Cambridge, 2007, pp. 35–36.

9 S. Gatland, "Designing Environments for Sound Control", in: *The American Institute of Architects.* www.aia.org/practicing/groups/kc/AIAB058394 (January 2, 2013).

10 J. D. Cutnell and K. W. Johnson, *Physics.* 4th ed. New York: 1998, pp. 466.

11 B. Blesser and L.-R. Salter, *op. cit.,* p. 11.

12 R. M. Schafer, *The Tuning of the World.* New York 1977, p. 222.

13 J. J. Gibson, *The Senses Considered as Perceptual Systems.* Boston 1966, p. 136.

14 M. A. A. Gutiérrez-Alonsa, F. Vexo and D. Thalmann, *Stepping into Virtual Reality.* London 2008, pp. 157–161.

15 *Ibid.*

16 Y.-F. Tuan, *Space and Place: The Perspective of Experience.* Minneapolis 1977, p. 11.

17 E. Harnett, "The Whole Package: The Relationship between Taste and Smell", in: *Serendip,* 2007. http://serendip.brynmawr.edu/exchange/node/1575 (December 14, 2014).

18 A. Barbara and A. Perliss, *Invisible Architecture: Experiencing Places through the Sense of Smell.* Milan 2006, p. 91.

19 N. Cheng, H. Cai and L. Belluscio, "*In Vivo* Olfactory Model of APP-Induced Neurodegeneration Reveals a Reversible Cell-Autonomous Function", in: *The Journal of Neuroscience,* September 28, 2011, pp. 31–39.

20 J. J. Gibson, *op. cit.,* p. 59.

21 E. Scherder, A. Bouma and L. Steen, "Effects of peripheral tactile nerve stimulation on affective behavior of patients with probable Alzheimer's disease", in: *American Journal of Alzheimer's Disease & Other Dementias,* March/April 1998, no. 13 (2), pp. 61–69.

22 E. T. Hall, *The Hidden Dimension. Man's Use of Space in Public and Private,* Garden City. New York 1969, p. 62.

23 B. Blesser and L.-R. Salter, *op. cit.,* p. 21.

block

and

quarter

With *Utopia*, Thomas More coined a term that architecture continues to strive for to the present day. Anon.: Città ideale, Italy, late 15th Century

a neighbourhood for a lifetime

Urban neighbourhoods for the elderly and people with dementia

Dieter Hoffmann-Axthelm

Of their towns, particularly of Amaurot

There lie gardens behind all their houses. These are large, but enclosed with buildings, that on all hands face the streets, so that every house has both a door to the street and a back door to the garden. Their doors have all two leaves, which, as they are easily opened, so they shut of their own accord; and, there being no property among them, every man may freely enter into any house whatsoever. At every ten years' end they shift their houses by lots.

They cultivate their gardens with great care [...] and there is, indeed, nothing belonging to the whole town that is both more useful and more pleasant. So that he who founded the town seems to have taken care of nothing more than of their gardens.

For they say the whole scheme of the town was designed at first by Utopus, but he left all that belonged to the ornament and improvement of it to be added by those that should come after him, that being too much for one man to bring to perfection.
Thomas More [1]

What makes a good neighbourhood? The true value of a residential neighbourhood only becomes apparent when there is an urgent need for more than the usual car parking, supermarkets and public transport link that the peripheral neighbourhoods of today's cities have to offer. It makes no difference whether the neighbourhood is a housing estate or private houses, or whether it lies in suburbia or in a village. Only then when the practical reasons for living on the outskirts prove just as

illusionary as the longing for green and the countryside, just as empty as the ideology of a modern living that befits one's social rank and as vacuous as the idealisation of the impractical and the unaesthetic that one agreed to or had to put up with, do we become aware of what makes a good neighbourhood. But there is also urgency in another respect: it is high time that state and municipal building policies respond to the urgent situation of those most affected. Instead of building more homes for the elderly and importing care staff from Eastern Europe, building policies, planning law, regional planning and state subsidies need to be revised in order, to put it bluntly, to upgrade and rebuild our cities to meet the needs of a large section of society that is rapidly approaching old age and to learn from the now widely acknowledged shortcomings of greenfield housing schemes. While the state spends its time adjusting pension schemes and care subsidies, they neglect to deal with the associated hardware, namely the need for an urban structure capable of providing for the needs of the elderly.

When people decide to move to the periphery, the decision is even now still couched in much varnishing of the truth. Whether motivated by a need to escape rising rent or house prices in the city, or whether it be the fulfilment of a life's dream, the decision is frequently so momentous, so intimately intertwined with personal self-conception, that it is defended against all doubts and contrary opinions for as long as possible. The straightforward assumption that a good neighbourhood is where one can feel at home for the rest of one's life is therefore largely irrelevant. For as long as one is healthy, has work and a car, there is no need to consider the negative aspects. Only when one becomes dependent, when one is ill, old, bedridden or dement do these aspects become unavoidable.

It seems, therefore, unlikely that a consensus among individual citizens will be reached. Only by distancing ourselves from such subjective motivations can we begin to ascertain what makes a good neighbourhood. For this, we need to stand back far enough to be able to consider the quite different needs of different age groups as well as to take into account the plethora of personal life stories in society. This we cannot achieve without adopting a professional viewpoint and making use of the respective necessary state or municipal regulations. While we are seeing a trend back towards the inner cities among the middle classes, we cannot rely on this. If left to market forces without the corrective intervention of public regulations, the result will be homogenous residential areas in the city while the socially disadvantaged remain in the periphery and those in need of care are forced into commercially run institutions.

A good neighbourhood is one that is good for all sections of society and age groups, regardless of people's individual fates and backgrounds. That the traditional urban structure – with its small-scale, individual plots and mix of typologies and different personalities brought about by private ownership – is optimal for immigrants from Eastern European cultures and

Living in the outskirts, whether in a home of one's own or in a large housing estate, gets more problematic as one grows older.

beyond, need no longer be questioned after five decades of work-motivated migration. This is the only way to maintain social diversity in the context of market economies, as the history of the 19th century already tells us: modern urban society, especially in large cities, paid a high price for the eradication of traditional structures based on the abstract egalitarian rationalism of modernism.

A similar pattern can be observed for the thresholds between age brackets. Middle-class parents believe they are improving the quality of life of their children when they move into a single-family home on the outskirts: better air quality, a natural environment, a garden for them to play in without needing to be watched over, less risk of traffic accidents, and a more like-minded social context are the much repeated motives. The disadvantages, although patently obvious to a neutral observer, are simply overlooked. The greatest deficit is a lack of experience. Those who live in large housing estates have little concrete experience of urban living, of contact to the world of employment, of familiarity with urban transport, of the adventure of discovering a city's functional niches in the homogenous environment of neighbourhoods of private houses where each keeps to their own, they also lack social interaction. Parents endeavour to compensate for this by ferrying their children back and forth – to and from kindergarten, school, sports practice, music lessons, ballet and so on. The children's natural environment is reduced to a monotonous succession of isolated walled gardens. And the mothers? If they do not accompany their menfolk into the city centres each morning, they remain at home, minding home and children, left behind as "green widows" hemmed in by the grass fringes separating the houses or the gardens of the terraces, unable to participate in the city and without opportunities for self-realisation.

The most extreme disadvantages of these conditions peculiar to living on the outskirts come with old age. As everything – daily errands and social contact – depends on being able to travel by car, private homes as well as large housing estates can rapidly become very isolating. And loneliness, as we know, can quickly lead to a sense of helplessness and from there to dementia. Lifts, letterboxes, green borders, parking spaces, circuitous access roads, supermarkets and shopping centres – everything that was practical about living on the outskirts – is suddenly dysfunctional as soon as physical mobility deteriorates. What was once so practical is now impractical; so impractical that those affected feel better looked-after elsewhere. The situation must be particularly difficult for elderly people who find themselves living in what has become the self-administered fortress of their private home. Housekeeping, tending to the garden, shopping, visiting doctors becomes a great effort. The city is far away and one has neither roots nor is one needed

As innumerable layers are placed one above the next, the cityscape becomes ever more monstrous. Julie Mehretu: "Berliner Plätze", 2008/09

Showing its expressive face: the façade of Casa Emilia in Solingen, Germany. Arbeitsgemeinschaft Großkemm/Richard + Monse/Molnar, 2007

by others in the neighbourhood. Suburban housing schemes do not teach people how to cooperate; just the contrary. Everyone is on their own, and all the more so when a partner dies, or the children are far away. There is no longer time to establish networks and to get to know places where growing older is easier to cope with. All that remains is to surrender oneself to the custody of the elderly care apparatus.

As society grows older as a whole, the ability to grow out of the conditions one steered towards earlier in life is no longer just a personal problem but also a social issue. Inner cities are similarly not without difficulties for old people: there are stairs to ascend, too few lifts, rising rent prices and the cost and effort of converting a bathroom, not to mention fraudsters preying on old people. Outside, uneven cobblestones are hard going for users of wheeled walkers, and black ice, fast traffic, unruly bicyclists and even young thieves present dangers for people with restricted mobility. But due to their concentration of functions and compact size, urban neighbourhoods also present a great opportunity to establish contacts, develop a network, to take part in everyday city life and to age gracefully without being dependent on the services of the social care industry.

Dense urban areas with a mix of uses do not in themselves guarantee that people can manage on their own as they grow older.

There is still a lot that must be provided through social help schemes, and these need to be established in advance. This cannot happen without investment in new facilities, such as a network of small local centres for expert care and medical assistance. More than anything, we need a shift in society towards more neighbourliness and the involvement of younger generations. The small-scale structure and social and functional mix of a heterogeneous urban neighbourhood is an ideal context in which this can arise. And it is also an indispensable instrument that allows people to still "make music" as they grow older.

The definitive turning point for self-reliant car-oriented lifestyles is the need for long-term care and the onset of dementia. Current estimates assume a long-term care period of on average ten years per person, and more in the future. Even with the current state of affairs, this presents a problem that will necessitate a change in thinking. This must start with those who are growing old now, as one cannot depend on younger people who are already stressed by their jobs, careers, children and relationships. The most valuable resource is probably those people who have reached retirement but are not yet in need of care or affected by dementia. At this age one is still strong enough to tackle new challenges and old and experienced enough to foresee one's own future by observing those

Marina di Corricella, the harbour of Procida, Italy, dates back to the 16th century. Its name comes from the Greek "kora calè" meaning nice quarter.

Although by no means barrier-free, living at close quarters creates chance encounters and encourages social interaction.

The residential building contains a good social mix of inhabitants. Tegeler Hafen, Berlin, Germany. moore ruble yudell architects and planners, 1984–1987

who are even older and often immobile and to practice for it, not least by helping others. The conventional systems for custodial care are too expensive, too anonymous and mechanised. And the closer one looks, the more nursing homes resemble places to die – "Lasciate ogni speranza, voi ch'entrate"![2]

The toughest test for the inclusion capacity of a neighbourhood is, of course, its ability to accommodate people with dementia. Those affected are often still physically mobile but no longer able to adequately direct their movement. They are dependent on the routines they have developed in earlier life. The ability to recall these routines from the depths of their memory can function correctly for as long as the environment is familiar and easy to manage, and provides unmistakable signals for actions, for example so that a door, a doorknob, a balustrade, a walkway, a pavement and so on are immediately recognisable as what they are and not complicated by digitally-operated technology, rendered invisible by design streamlining, severely damaged, in a stage of conversion or obstructed by some other careless lack of attention. People with dementia are best able to cope with their environment, when the signs within it, the heights, sizes and appearances of the relevant elements, correspond to how they knew them to be when they established their routines – when they are constant and easy to grip, and are reliably maintained as such.

So, what makes a good neighbourhood? As banal as it may sound, we find ourselves referring back to some of the most generally applicable insights. The ABC of the mixed city is therefore not new:

– a sufficiently small-scale urban grain through the statutory regulation of plot sizes
– a range of house owners and backgrounds

– statutory regulation and grant subsidisation to ensure social and functional diversity
– traffic policies that resist the dominance of cars and create networks of spaces rather than segregating traffic into fast transit arteries and separate protected zones
– the highly individualised usability of public spaces and green areas

In addition there are a number of necessary procedural prerequisites: there has to be a consensus in municipal politics and the provision of sufficient time for participation processes and unorthodox financing models.

How can architecture contribute? In terms of the structure of buildings, architects must demonstrate the will to apply as much professional energy as they usually do for the design to the creation of a range of different typologies. The removal of obstructions and thresholds is only one aspect of this. Architects must also ask themselves how their design contributes to nearness, neighbourliness, interaction, and how it facilities being seen and heard? In these respects, too, we are still very much at the beginning.

In today's day and age, mobility impairments and dementia must be recognised as common public conditions and should not be hidden. Nevertheless, it is not always possible to make a public space sufficiently safe and legible for every possible user, even though it is important that people come out of their closed environment and take part in public space and life. There have to be zones that are more protected.

That does not mean that we should immediately embark on creating generously-sized protected areas for movement that are removed from traffic zones. Proximity and comprehensibility

The arrangement of the 81 buildings adapts and improves on the concept of parallel rows of housing. Buchheimer Weg Estate, Cologne, Germany. ASTOC – Architects und Planners, 2008–2012

Eight residents live in a residential group for people with dementia on the ground floor of one of the houses with outpatient support and a sheltered outdoor area of their own.

are still the most important spatial criteria for establishing social contacts. Communal green spaces that no one makes use of, such as the green spaces trapped within perimeter block structures or between orthogonally arranged rows of buildings, are neither helpful for orientation nor uplifting; this we need to avoid. The neighbourhood is more important than providing residents with a sweeping view. As the radius of activity of old people starts to diminish, areas rich in building structure become more helpful and stimulating: a sensible mixture of building constellations with side wings and rearward buildings, interspersed with small-scale green spaces and structured by helpful and unequivocal edges that correspond to age-old neighbourhood boundaries.

Finally, we must not forget that all good intentions still have to be economically feasible. In socio-economic and urban terms, there is a direct correspondence between the cost of land and care costs, regardless of how in future the trend towards reintegrating care into the family will be achieved organisationally. Density is not only an important human resource but also an economic one.

1   T. More: *Utopia*, 1901 Project Gutenberg.

2   "Abandon all hope, you who enter here." The last verse of the inscription over the entrance to Inferno in D. Alighieri's *Divine Comedy*.

Hanging out in their hammocks, visitors to the house-like structure are at once apart from but still part of the public space. Heri&Salli: "Flederhaus" on the forecourt of the Museum quarter in Vienna, Austria, 2011

Journeying to other places. As an oasis in the bustle of the city and a landmark in the urban landscape, the "Flederhaus" exemplifies the sensory design of public spaces.

meaningful outdoor spaces for people with dementia

Annette Pollock

When talking about outdoor spaces for people with dementia, many people refer to them as "sensory" gardens – but this is only one of the many facets that contribute to a successful and well-designed outdoor space. Gardens and other outdoor areas need to be much more than just sensory spaces – they need to be meaningful, understandable and safe, as well as provide for pleasure, socialising and activity.

If we live into our 90s, approximately a third of us will have dementia – and this will represent a complete cross-section of society, dementia is not selective. As such, the designer of outdoor spaces for people with dementia needs to consider the background and interests of the users as well as cater for the known disabilities of older people in general and specifically those with dementia. In the UK, two thirds of people with dementia live in the community while one third live in care homes.

Firstly, let us deal with the practical side – the design essentials, whether it is for a care home, hospital ward or private garden. Most of the following attributes also apply to public parks and gardens too.

A good microclimate

By this, we mean a sunny area, sheltered from wind and noise and with some areas of shade too; a place where the older person feels comfortable and not threatened. Wind is particularly bothersome as it can blow frail people over and also lowers the ambient temperature. Of course, a gentle breeze on a hot day is desirable.

A secure environment

This means a place from which people with dementia cannot "escape" into a potentially harmful environment. Gates leading out from this secure environment need to be carefully concealed to avoid attracting the person with dementia, as a locked gate can cause much frustration and stress.

A safe place with easy access

This means barrier-free access, level and non-slip surfacing, no gradients in the grass and planting areas that could cause someone to fall over and handrails when required to help people on their way. As part of being barrier-free, there should be no sharply contrasting colours in the surfacing or at the door threshold, as people with visuoperceptual problems may see

Barrier-free walkway beneath a pergola. Cherish Yearn Membership Senior Retirement Community, Shanghai, China

Conceived as a club with its own membership. The comfortable senior retirement community is reserved for Chinese civil servants.

The one- and two-person apartments are pre-furnished with basic furnishings and can be rented for independent or assisted living.

Outdoor activities are a key part of the Green Care Concept. Lillevang house, Farum, Denmark. Landscape architects Landskab & Rum ApS, 1998

Wheelchair-accessible raised plant beds in the senior residence at Stavangerstrasse 26, Berlin, Germany. Harms Wulf Landschaftsarchitekten, 2005

Fruit and vegetable garden at the Kompetenzzentrum für Menschen mit Demenz, Nuremberg, Germany. Feddersen Architekten, 2006

this as a step or change in level and consequently hesitate, potentially leading to a fall. Similarly, services covers in hard surfacing can be a visual barrier and need to be disguised by using covers into which the surface material can be inset.

An "indoor-outdoor" area

It is very useful to have an intermediate space that is covered, to provide for sitting out on a day when the weather is not so good – and to provide a space outdoors for activities such as potting up plants, painting, having a coffee and so on. This kind of space provides shelter and shade – and if well designed can also help to prevent glare within the building from the sun when it is at a low inclination. Next, how do we furnish the space?

Seats, tables, gazebos, pergolas, arches

Timber is a good material for seats, being warm, quick to dry and usually traditional in appearance. Seats need to be robust, stable and comfortable with arms that aid sitting and rising. They should be located at regular intervals to encourage walking from one place to the next.

Tables and parasols allow for informal socialising and recreation. A covered feature such as a gazebo acts as a destination point to go to – and to participate in activities. Raised planters of differing heights allow people to work at them whether standing or seated. A garden shed is a place in which to potter. Pergolas can provide an attractive arch to go through, directing movement – and if large enough may also provide shelter from the sun when the plants have grown over them.

Plants

Any plants in a garden for people with dementia must be safe – that is, not harmful in any way. Edible plants are good to have, such as apples, herbs and berries. Plants that can trigger memory are particularly useful for stimulating conversation – how many little girls have played with fuchsia flowers making them into ballerinas? Made daisy chains? How many children have picked apples to eat? Have smelled mint or lavender? We also recognise the changing seasons through plants, spring bulbs, summer flowers, autumn colours, falling leaves – and this helps to keep people in the "real world".

Meaningful activity

There are many things that take place outside: planting and then harvesting the fruit and vegetables, having family parties, playing games (putting, croquet, ball games), working in the shed on woodwork, mending things, tinkering with the bicycle, looking after chickens or rabbits, feeding the birds, hanging out the washing and so on. All of these promote activity and actively encourage memory and discussion. Some of us welcome group activity – whereas others prefer to sit alone, smelling the plants and enjoying a light breeze on the face. Access to outdoor space at upper levels – be it a balcony or a roof terrace – is important too. Other cultures may use spaces differently and have other associations with it. For example, for aboriginal people in Australia, the outdoors is where home is – being inside is only for shelter.

So why is all this so important? Because we need to keep older people and people with dementia as healthy and happy as possible – and also keep them in the real world as long as we can. With an increasingly ageing population, the costs of care are an enormous consideration. Taking exercise and getting vitamin D have been shown in numerous studies to be extremely important in maintaining good physical health, in preventing falls and also in maintaining cognition. Happy people are easier to care for, and an open door to the outside can reduce behaviour that challenges and stresses. And let us not forget those who care for people with dementia – if the people with dementia are happier and easier to look after, the carers will benefit as well.

Outdoor areas with covered walkway between the buildings in the background. Hanna Reemtsma House, Hamburg, Germany. Schneekloth + Partner, 2011

Light- and air-permeable walls provide a sense of enclosure and obviate the need for railings. Centre for Geriatric Psychiatry in Pfäfers, Switzerland. huggenbergerfries Architekten, 2010

kahla housing for the elderly

Kahla, Germany

Architects
Jörg Lammert
GEROTEKTEN
Plannungsbüro für
soziale Aufgaben

Client
Diakonie
Ost-Thüringen
Wohn- und
Seniorenzentrum
Käthe Kollwitz
gGmbH

Planning
08/2006–08/2007

Construction
12/2008–02/2010

Gross floor area
4,400 m²

The residents of the new "Seniorensiedlung" project in the town of Kahla live in the heart of an intact residential urban neighbourhood next to a school, a playing field and a supermarket. The internal arrangement of the building was designed from the outset to counteract isolation and loneliness of the residents. This applies both to the compact flats in the three pavilion-like low buildings with gardens as well as the communal housing building.

The building is structured around seven compact courtyard spaces with a cloister-like walkway around them inviting one to either cross (square) or settle in them (garden). The courtyards correspond to different types of social spaces and as such structure the complex into notional neighbourhoods. The design creates an environment for six residential groups arranged on two floors around a leafy courtyard. These dense clusters in turn open onto the communal courtyards and the pergola court, which are used by all the residents in the complex.

Each of the residential groups has a large living and dining area with a kitchen for their day-to-day activities. This central element defines the rest of the structure of the building. Light wells, created by incisions cut into the volume of the building create transitional spaces between indoors and outdoors and allow daylight to spill into the interior.

Outbuildings and courtyards structure the accommodation buildings into social units. As part of this, the planting of the green areas is tailored to the specific needs of the residents. In two sheltered gardens, there are beds that the residents can plant and tend on their own. The gardens are enclosed by greenery around their perimeter so that people with dementia can go for walks on their own without wandering off. Each courtyard has a specific botanic character and existing mature trees have been incorporated into the gardens.

The architectural concept focuses on the needs of the elderly residents and attempts to develop a functional and considered plan that caters for the wishes and particular needs of the residents. Daily life is oriented around much the same pattern as it would be in one's own home, and additional assistance with everyday tasks is provided according to the respective resources and interests of the residents, and their biographical backgrounds. A special aspect of the housing scheme in Kahla is its lighting concept. A combination of natural daylight, glare-free artificial light and indirect lighting ensures that the rooms are optimally illuminated. The interiors are bright and spacious and orange is used throughout the buildings to create a friendly atmosphere. A further aspect of the colour concept is the colour coding of the living rooms to give them a specific identity and provide orientation.

Sheltered courtyard with beech tree

Greened courtyard with protected water basin

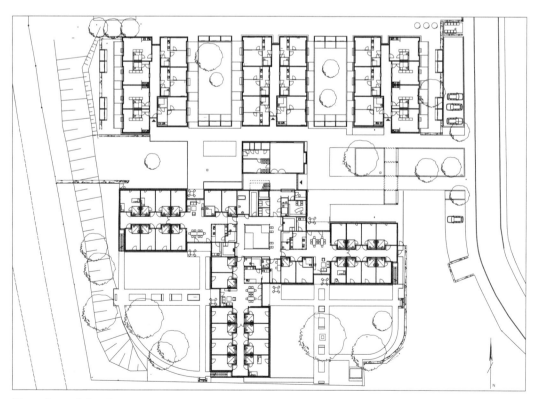

Floor plan and site plan

Wardrobe, kitchen and pantry – just like in a "normal" house

Colour coded interiors help provide orientation.

zollikofen nursing and care centre for the elderly

Zollikofen, Switzerland

Client
Arthur Waser Gruppe

Preliminary planning
ARGE
Feddersen Architekten/
stankovic architekten,
Berlin, Germany

Design
Feddersen Architekten,
Berlin, Germany

Construction
ARGE
Feddersen Architekten/
IAAG Architekten AG,
Bern, Switzerland

Planning
since 2010

Completion
2016

Gross floor area
20,500 m²

Although outpatient care programmes are becoming increasingly relevant, nursing and care homes remain an important part of the spectrum of care provision for the elderly. In future, we can expect to see homes become part of a socially mixed centre of a locality: in addition to providing nursing care, there will also be separate apartments, either in-house or in the vicinity, as well as medical services, food and shopping facilities. As the demand for inpatient care is hard to predict in the long term, new building concepts will therefore need to be flexible.

In Zollikofen, a neighbourhood just outside Bern, a new nursing and care centre for the elderly is being built that incorporates these ideas from the outset. Located just a few minutes on foot from the local S-Bahn station, its residents can travel easily to the centre of Bern with its shops and to the university, which offers a programme of courses for mature students. The new building is located in the centre of Zollikofen and has been designed with future flexibility in mind. This is made possible by a modular structure that consists of six pavilion-like buildings linked to one another by a main central axis. The residents' rooms are arranged along a meandering path that winds its way through the different pavilions. The floor plans of the nursing area employ the same underlying grid as a group of four two-room apartments, and structural walls have been kept to a minimum. This makes it possible to vary the proportion of nursing care places and apartments at a later date by making a few straightforward alterations. Rooms can be joined together and the bathrooms can be converted into small kitchens. In total, the complex will contain rooms for 172 residents in nursing care and 58 apartments.

This inclusive model will, however, only be successful if the apartments are not perceived as being part of the nursing home. The design of the interiors must therefore create the impression of separate units, each with their own address. Separate stairs and lifts ensure that the day-to-day paths of the two groups of residents do not overlap.

On the ground floor, service facilities are available for all the residents as well as for local inhabitants from the surrounding district. The concept includes a medical centre, a chemist, a library, a restaurant as well as space for shops and services that help to establish the complex as a new centre within its surroundings. This modular concept allows the centre to provide a broad range of elderly care services and supporting facilities under one roof: from independent living to round-the-clock nursing care as well as hybrid forms such as sheltered housing or day care.

The courtyard on the Bernstrasse is the main entrance for the entire complex.

Site plan

Main foyer and reception

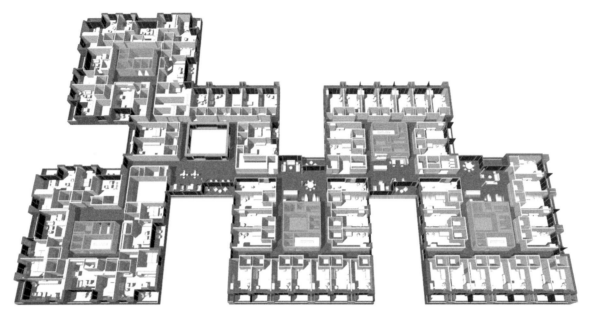

Isometric view showing the meandering layout

Every nursing care group has its own communal area with direct access to the balcony.

Communal lobbies on the floors with assisted living apartments provide an attractive and comfortable place for residents to meet and chat.

Outdoor spaces can be used by both residents and the public.

home for the elderly and library

Zaragoza, Spain

Architects
Carroquino/Finner
Arquitectos

Client
Ayuntamiento de
Zaragoza, Suelo y
Vivienda de Aragón

Planning
06/2005–08/2006

Construction
10/2006–04/2008

Gross floor area
3,020 m²

The Benjamín Jarnés Library, located in the Actur District in Zaragoza, suffered from a lack of space and could no longer adequately fulfil its functions. Based on a recommendation from the Board of Trustees of Zaragoza, the construction of a new socio-cultural building was proposed where the library was to be relocated. In order to use human as well as material resources efficiently, it was agreed that the new building to be created should house both a centre for the elderly and the Benjamín Jarnés Library.

The volume consists of three levels and a basement and used prefabrication to minimise construction time, cost and constructions errors. It is organised around an open central court that houses the vertical communication elements and provides the building with sufficient daylight. Service areas are organised vertically aiming to reduce cost and simplify the installation of service ducts.

Rooms intended for the elderly were located close to the street level, facilitating their access. The lobby acts as a big space communicating the interior of the building with the two parallel streets and creating a continuation of the outer public space into the building. The assembly hall is situated close to the main entrance, next to a multipurpose room that offers the possibility to host activities in connection to the main auditorium.

Another characteristic of the project is its adaptability and flexibility. Due to its organisation, it is possible to open and close rooms without interfering with the general circulation of the building. As mentioned above, the areas of the building to be used by the elderly are located on the lower levels; the exercise room is in the basement, the assembly hall on the ground floor and lecture rooms and workshop rooms on the second level. Classrooms and workshop spaces are divided through adjustable partitions that provide flexible environments.

The minimal number of openings on the façade allows a higher degree of climatic control within the building. The courtyard, on the other hand, allows bigger openings through a curtain wall system with thermal bridge breaks and Low-E coating glass.

Exterior view of the entrance to the library

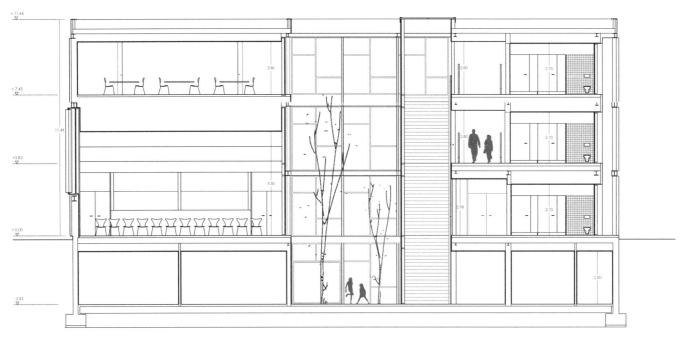

Section through the library and multifunctional spaces

Spacious entrance area

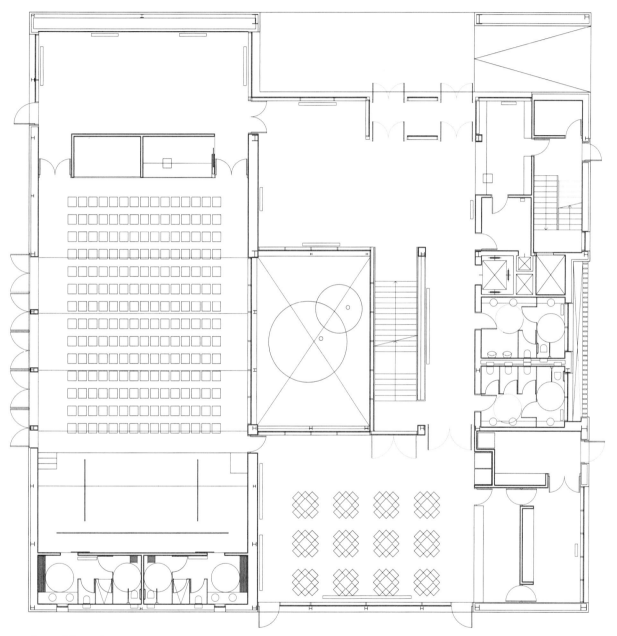

Ground floor plan

Central atrium

Different materials define the different sections of the façade.

vialonga elderly day care centre

Lisbon, Portugal

Architetcs
Miguel Arruda
Arquitectos
Associados Lda./
Miguel Arruda

Client
TNS 3

Planning
07/2005–06/2007

Construction
04/2007–02/2008

Gross floor area
600 m²

The elderly day care centre is located in a peripheral area of Lisbon, inserted in a context that displays all the common defects of suburban clusters near big cities. The population is essentially divided into two distinct groups. The first comprises the working population, the other group are non-working elderly people who divide their time between being with their families and meeting friends, neighbours and acquaintances in the coffee shops of the neighbourhood and in the few available green areas; here they visit with each other, debate politics or play cards.

The day care centre is the result of efforts by local authorities to create a space for this second group – the elderly population – and offer them a place for social interaction that includes comfort needs such as a cafeteria, a room for health care needs or a barber shop. Formally and conceptually, the intention was to create a singular architectural object. In the given social, cultural and urban context, the day care centre appears as a reference point, contrasting with the surrounding buildings through form and scale.

Beginning with a pure box, the architects gave each elevation of the volume a different height, thus creating an interior with varying ceiling heights, depending on programmatic function. On the exterior, they achieved a formal dimension that is characterised by non-orthogonal façades, yet creates a "traditional" roof with two slopes. In the centre of the building a courtyard has been substracted from the volume that interacts with almost all interior spaces and provides natural lighting and ventilation. The walls of the north elevation are inflected towards the interior in order to allow covered access to those who arrive by vehicle, which is often the case with elderly persons. This generous space marks the building's main entrance and provides welcome protection in case of adverse weather conditions.

From the beginning the architects' intention was to lend a distinct character to the building's exterior by using a uniform material that would cover wall as well as roof surfaces, thereby providing this architectural piece with a certain abstractness. The aim was to counteract stereotypical images of what an "old-age retirement home" is like. The building's architectural features, inside and outside, have come to be very much appreciated by those who use the centre on a regular basis. The building's appearance is supposed to mirror the desire for recognition on the part of its users and their wish to play a role in the social and cultural regeneration of this degraded suburban area.

View from the north of the main entrance

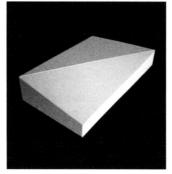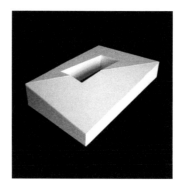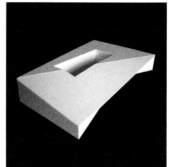

Conceptual study

Covered entrance area

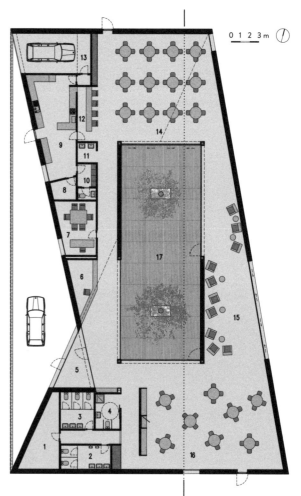

0 1 2 3m

Floor plan and spatial concept

1	Store	9	Kitchen
2	WC men	10	Wardrobe
3	WC women	11	Washroom
4	WC disabled	12	Bar
5	Entrance	13	Garage
6	Reception	14	Dining room
7	Consultation room	15	Lounge
8	Store	16	Activity room
		17	Open courtyard

Open rectangular internal courtyard

Light-coloured façade on the south side of the building

Views from inside of the surroundings

Orange surfaces in the interior contrast with the white walls.

de hogeweyk

Village for people
with dementia

De Hogeweyk, Netherlands

Architects
Dementia Village
Architects,
Netherlands

Interior design
Verpleegehuis
Hogewey and
Dementia Village
Architects,
Netherlands

Client
Hogewey Vivium
Zorggoep,
Netherlands

Completion
Phase I:
04/2008
Phase II:
12/2009

Gross floor area
11,500 m²

"Debatable in theory – true to life in practice" is how one could summarise the De Hogeweyk project. Here the focus lies not on care or nursing for the elderly but on living, supplemented by individual care services as needed. Although the residents cannot leave the actual site, they are able to move around freely within its confines. Inside De Hogeweyk there is a supermarket, a doctor's surgery, hairdresser, restaurant, a theatre, small shops and various club rooms – in short a microcosm of the world outside. The Dutch Alzheimer's Foundation has praised the facility, which is the first of its kind, as a "pioneering" model project.

The site in Weesp, a small suburban municipality southwest of Amsterdam, is the size of an urban block and covers a total area of 15,000 m². The perimeter of the block is lined by two-storey buildings containing a total of 23 apartments which have been clad with different surface materials to create the impression of a series of terraced houses, echoing the buildings in the surroundings.

The interior of the block is structured by a series of small outdoor courtyards, green areas, gardens and a central "boulevard", which contains shops and a doctor's surgery that serves the residents. On the upper floor, walkways provide a horizontal connection between the different areas while lifts and stairs connect the levels vertically. The main entrance serves as a kind of "security gate" so that staff can intercept residents before they leave the site and lead them back into the residential group.

Each apartment houses six to seven residents who are assisted by a permanent team of care and nursing staff, with two members of staff – not in uniform – present in an apartment at the same time. The concept is similar to that of a residential group, focussing on everyday activities and normal living patterns in which residents can do as they please or take part in communal activities. The apartments have been designed to correspond to seven different typical lifestyles, each with different floor plans, materials and colours. This lifestyle approach caters for people with different cultural backgrounds, different manners of speech and different patterns of social interaction.

Despite the diverse living concepts, all the buildings, paths and squares look onto one another. The clarity of the environment and the variety of different impressions help promote orientation and a feeling of normality. By using real materials for the building, the designers minimise the sense of artificiality of the surroundings. Likewise, everything else appears to be "real": for example, the supermarket sells proper fresh produce for the residents. For the initiators, the project has already successfully demonstrated their vision of a de-institution-alised living environment for people with dementia. Nevertheless, they feel there is still room for improvement and a follow-up project is currently being considered for a neighbouring site.

Greened residential courtyard

The south face of the urban block is a single closed frontage designed to look like brick-clad terraced houses.

Bird's-eye view showing the surrounding buildings

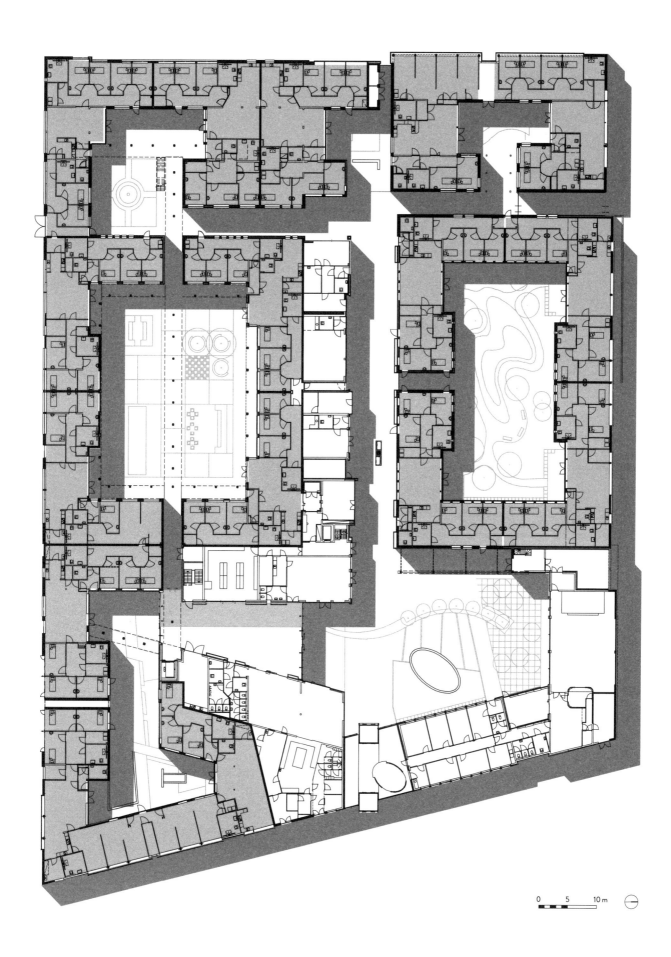

Floor plan of the entire complex showing how the buildings enclose and define the courtyards and public spaces

0   5   10 m

Space for gardening

Courtyard with planted beds

"Homely" living style

"Cultural" living style

"Wealthy" living style

urban game-board

Dementia and urban game design perspectives

Eleni Kolovou

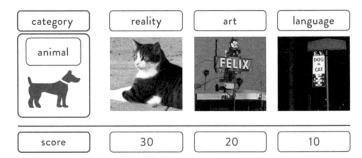

category	reality	art	language
animal			

score	30	20	10

In user tests with people with slight dementia, research is being conducted into whether suitably designed smartphone apps can help provide better orientation.

The city-dwellers' experience of the urban space is currently being augmented through the presence of information and communication technologies (ICT). Spatial awareness is being filtered through channels of data dissemination, wireless networks and information dynamics. Consequently, the social core encountered in the public space is rapidly evolving into a digitally interactive community who is developing relationships sharing spatial and information consciousness. This evolution though, is synchronous to another significant change in the city context; the fact that the citizens inhabiting this evolving space are getting older. The demographic ageing is setting a challenging field for urban design accentuating issues of safety, accessibility and social inclusion. "Topographical disorientation", described in the work of Pai and Jacobs[1] as a difficulty in orienting to, navigating through and feeling familiar with one's surroundings, observed in Alzheimer's disease (AD) has been an important issue in urban design. Although the adaptation of architecture and urban design to the needs of people with mental or cognitive impairments has been addressed in the past, the incorporation of ICT networks in the urban space towards the same needs is yet to be further explored.

Public space, both as an entirety of visual stimuli, as well as a field where city experience takes place, is strongly connected with the notion of "play" in literature. The act of playing in the theory of the *Situationalists* appears to be among the core

social activities, that takes place at any given moment within the urban space. According to Stevens "urban spatial form creates conditions of chance which engender various kinds of playful activity".[2] The concept of play is not disregarded either in the treatment of dementia as cognitively stimulating leisure activities may delay the onset of dementia in community-dwelling elders.[3] Currently, researchers are evaluating the potential of close-to-reality simulations and generic video games to stimulate the cognitive abilities of AD patients.[4] Consequently, the game as a process of recollection and identification offers a broad field of experimentation concerning perception of the urban space, creation of memories, landmarking and wayfinding in the city - issues that are of great importance for people with dementia.

As the public expression of play reflects the dynamics of a complex multilayered urban reality, games adapt to the current situation and the users of public space become increasingly engaged in mobile technology leisure activities. However, the emergence of mobile devices has a significant impact on the healthcare system as well; mobile applications and services are increasingly being adopted by the health delivery system for chronic disease management or as assistance for the elderly.[5] In the field of dementia care research patients and caregivers are introduced to innovative methods based on mobile technology; GPS tracking, route-planning are some of

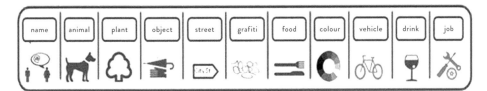

Reality, art and language denote the three levels from which the users can call up information.

the emergent issues in this field along with games of memory and association. In this case, an adaptation of a hybrid urban game, *CITYgories*,[6] is being explored as a link between the city and memory using mobile technology as a medium.

CITYgories is a digital re-interpretation of the word-game of categories set at an urban scale. The game sees the city as an urban game board; the player is called to interact with a familiar environment in an inventive way dealing with a process of unpredictable encounters as such in the context of a city. The urban web is decoded and fragmented into categories from the player's point of view. The platform of the game provides the digital space where data from the physical space is classified as the players go through a mental process of observation, recollection and analysis. Mobile phones are suggested as tools for an immediate gameplay. The quality of information in the user's generated content is divided into three levels: reality, art and language. The scope of the game includes words being sought as physical entities in the public space, as represented in illustration in public media, or typed in advertisement and public signage. The complexity of the stimuli in the competing material is coded in hierarchy based on the level of information the element embeds and this has also been used as an evaluation system in the grading stage. The reference game, *CITYgories*, is to be used as a playful framework for the study and the game's platform and interface will be accordingly modified to address the needs of the research.

Within the game lies an alternative perspective of what is commonly named as a "trivial" environment. In this case spatial experience is addressed at as a goal-oriented game process, where players are called to wander in the city in an attempt to fulfil their quest as a "technique of locomotion".[7] This method could provide a common ground for people with dementia and their caregivers in mapping and visualising routes since research has revealed that dementia patients tend to use visual references and landmarks as wayfinding techniques rather than maps or written directions. In collaboration with the Greek Federation of Alzheimer's Disease, play-tests will be carried out in several dementia care day centres with the participation of patients with mild dementia or mild cases of cognitive disorder. The outcome of the play-tests will be evaluated in order to assess the contribution of the game to the patients' orientation and cognitive abilities. The material collected will offer a ground to study the perception of the urban space through the eyes of people who face memory and orientation disabilities. The play-tests will help to establish a framework of further development concerning the interactive game in favour of the patient's abilities. The process of recording and recalling memories by using a smartphone as an intuitive mapping device is to be examined as a potential medium of turning the cityscape itself into a compass for people at early stages of dementia.

1   M. C. Pai and W. J. Jacobs, "Topographical disorientation in community-residing patients with Alzheimer's disease", in: *International Journal of Geriatric Psychiatry*, 19 (2004), pp. 250–255.

2   Q. Stevens, *The Ludic City: Exploring the Potential of Public Spaces.* London 2007, p. 38.

3   T. N. Akbaraly et al., "Leisure activities and the risk of dementia in the elderly: results from the Three-City Study", in: *Neurology*, September 15; 73 (2009), 11, pp. 854–861.

4   F. Imbeault, B. Bouchard and A. Bouzouane, *Serious games in cognitive training for Alzheimer's patients, Serious Games and Applications for Health* (SeGAH), 2011 IEEE 1st International Conference, pp. 1–8.

5   D. H. West, "How mobile devices are transforming healthcare", in: *Issues in Technology Innovation*, 18 (2012), pp. 1–14.

6   http://citygoriesgame.com/, 2012, game design by bIZZ (A. Kolovou and E. Kolovou) web-development by G. Karpathios and A. Pantelis. "Best in Fest" award in Athens Plaython festival, 2012. Presented at GameCity 7 and I-Tag Exhibition Conference in Nottingham, 2012.

7   J. Fillon, "New Games", in: U. Conrads (ed.), *Programs and manifestoes on 20th-century architecture.* Cambridge, Mass. 1975, p. 155.

town

and

country

Embedded in village surroundings. Centre for Geriatric Psychiatry in Pfäfers, Switzerland. huggenbergerfries Architekten, 2010

mapping dementia

How can we prepare for tomorrow? What do we need to plan for?

Sabine Sütterlin

Places for memories

My grandparents' living room no longer exists, although the house is still there in the industrial Rhine harbour district of Kleinhüningen in Basel and has since been refurbished and converted. All the same, I can still clearly remember how their "parlour" was furnished, how it smelt and what the half-linen cushions felt like on the bed sofa in the corner that I slept on when I visited my grandparents during the holidays.

The living room was on the third floor. One day my grandmother entered the room just as my grandfather was about to climb out of the window. With quite some persuasion, she was able to hold him back. "He got a little muddled," was what I was told later. He thought he was in the single-storey workers' cottage of his childhood where he and his brother often used to climb out of the window into the courtyard behind.

At that time in the early 1980s, no one spoke of dementia. The term "Alzheimer's" first became more widely known towards the end of that decade, having made its way back to Europe from the USA: the term itself originated in Europe at the beginning of the 20th century when the German neurologist Alois Alzheimer first described the disease. Only later did it come to be commonly known by the more general term "dementia".

My family responded to my grandfather's strange behaviour with a mixture of amusement and concern, and it was generally taken to be a moment of temporary confusion. In autumn 1984 he died aged 89. Only one year later, my grandmother went into hospital after breaking her thighbone, and died a few months later. During this period she only occasionally

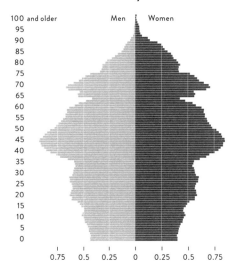

Germany 2008

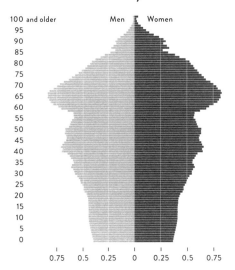

Germany 2030

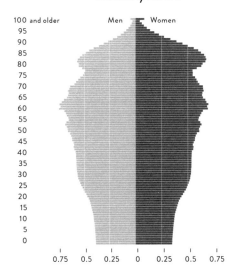

Germany 2050

Composition of the population according to age in Germany in 2008, 2030 and 2050 in percent (data basis: Federal Statistical Office, 12th coordinated population projection Variant 1–W2)

recognised her children and grandchildren. Her hands, which had spent a lifetime constantly doing something – cooking, gardening, knitting, sewing or looking after someone who was ill – now busied themselves with taking one paper tissue after another from a box and tearing it into neat strips.

Towards the end of his 88 years, my uncle, my mother's brother, also had difficulties recognising his nearest relatives. His wife recounted that he would sit at his desk with a vacant look and shift pieces of paper back and forth before finally realising that he could make no sense of them, whereupon he would break off saying: "Come on, let's go for a drive."

Nearly everyone has a similar story to tell of old people in their extended family, or have at least heard them from friends and acquaintances. And we will hear them more often. The probability of developing dementia rises from the age of 65 and becomes more critical from the age of 80. Currently every 20th person in Germany is over 80 years old. The rapid ageing of society in Germany will mean that by 2030, every 13th person will be over 80 years old, by 2050 every seventh.

At some point before then – assuming I conform to the statistical life expectancy of my age group – I will reach very old age and may perhaps also start to lose my memory. Which of the many places I have lived in will I remember? And how many people will be familiar with the places in my memory?

The Berlin Institute for Population and Development has analysed these developments in its "Dementia Report", focussing especially on the individual regions of Germany, Austria and Switzerland. This article summarises the most important findings. The full report is available online from www.berlin-institut.org.

As the population grows older, there will be more people with dementia
The probability of developing dementia increases with age. The only exception to this is the hereditary form of Alzheimer's which can develop before the age of 60. This is, however, extremely rare. To date there is no unequivocal evidence that old people in certain regions, cultures or peoples are less prone to developing dementia than their counterparts elsewhere. But when the population as a whole ages, so too does the proportion of people who suffer from dementia.

According to Alzheimer's Disease International (ADI), the overall proportion of people with dementia around the world in 2009 was 4.7 %. The highest proportion, 7.2 %, was found in Western Europe: the lowest, 1.2 %, in West Africa.

Nevertheless, even now the poorer nations already account for more than half of all people with dementia due to the sheer size of their populations. These countries are presently comparatively young, but they too will age. As countries become more developed, the birth rate typically falls while life expectancy rises. And this process is happening much faster in the developing countries than it did in the industrialised nations.

The proportion of people with dementia in developing nations and emerging economies will therefore also increase, albeit later but then more rapidly and in greater numbers. According to the ADI's calculations in 2009, the number of people with dementia until 2030 will rise most dramatically in countries with low and medium earnings whose populations continue to grow. The highest rates of growth are expected in North Africa and the Middle East, followed by Latin America and South and East Asia. By 2050, 70 % of all people with dementia may be living in poorer countries.[1]

Europe is ageing and shrinking
As a consequence of consistently low birth rates over a period of decades, many parts of Europe are already beginning to shrink, for example in Germany, Italy, the Baltic states and large parts of Eastern and Southern Europe. Immigration can no longer compensate for this decline in the birth rate.

Germany and Italy now have the oldest populations in Europe. In both countries, the number of over-65-year-olds accounts for a good 20 % of the population, which is considerably more than the West European average of 18 % and the industrial nation average of 16 %. In North America the proportion is currently 13 %, in China 9 % and in developing and emerging nations, on average 5 %. Only one country is older: in Japan, 24 % of the population are already over 65 years old.[2]

When baby boomers reach retirement age
The challenges that the ageing and shrinking of the population will bring in future – not just but also as a result of dementia – can be shown clearly using Germany as an example.

The majority of the current generation of over-65-year-olds in Germany have paid social insurance for years and were able to put aside savings during the period of rebuilding after the war and the economic miracle.[3] These pensioners have a comparatively good chance of receiving good care when they become frail or demented and in need of care. Currently the high-birth-rate years of the baby boomer generation – the nearly

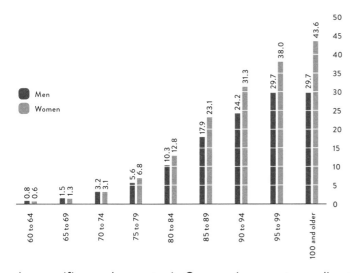

Age-specific prevalence rates in Germany in percent according to gender[4]

1.2 million children born each year between 1959 and 1968 in the two German territories – dominate society. Today they are "in their prime" and represent a significant proportion of the working population, and therefore pay into the social insurance system. As professional care staff, they look after older people, and as daughters, sons or children-in-law, they are increasingly called on to look after their older relatives.

In about 2030, the baby boomers will reach their 65th birthday. Thereafter follows a veritable inversion of the population pyramid as more and more people reach this age. Almost twice as many people were born in 1964 than in any of the years of the 1980s. From 2030 onwards, they will be the cause of "major challenges for the pension and health insurance systems, but they will also add a new dimension to the image of old age," as detailed in a "demographic portrait" by the German Centre of Gerontology (DZA).[5] In Germany, the baby boomers also have less in the way of savings than their parents do today: by the time they reach retirement, there is not so much to share around. According to estimates by the German Institute for Economic Research, the pension entitlement of many people may already fall beneath what is needed to cover basic needs by 2020, especially in the former East German states.[6] According to the "German Ageing Survey" (DEAS), a nationwide study that periodically surveys people in the second half of life, it is likely that fewer and fewer people will be able to fall back on private savings to compensate for the loss of income resulting from low pension entitlement.[7]

The balance between young and old will only start to swing back slightly after 2050 when the baby boomer generations reach the end of their lifetime and the following lower-birth-rate generations reach retirement age.

As the probability of developing dementia increases from the age of 65 onwards, the rise in incidences of the disease can be predicted relatively accurately based on the number of births in those years. Calculations undertaken by the Fritz Beske Institute of Research on Public Health Care indicate that the number of dementia patients in Germany could increase from 1.1 million in 2007 to approximately double that number by 2050. However, as the overall population in Germany will have shrunk to around 69 million by that time, the relative increase amounts to 144 %.[8]

Town and country

How well people with dementia will fare in future depends on where they live. Dementia is not more common in the country than in an urban environment, but the challenges that dementia presents are greatest in regions where the population is already growing older and where there has been an exodus of young people, leaving behind elderly people, some of whom are at risk of poverty. In these sparsely populated areas it is difficult to sustain an adequate level of health care, as doctors are unwilling to move there. And where municipalities are already constrained by budget deficits, they are even less likely to have sufficient financial resources in future than other regions.

The "Dementia Distribution Map" shows how the present and projected incidence of dementia matches the current and future population distribution in 2025 in the different regions of Germany, Austria and Switzerland. Both of these predominantly German-speaking neighbours have a younger population. Nevertheless, they can expect to see the same developments in future.

In Germany, the former East German states of the country are most affected. A similar pattern, albeit on a smaller scale, can also be seen in the regions bordering the former iron curtain in Austria. Likewise the rural areas at the edge of the Alps where many residents have moved to larger agglomerations, are also struggling to cope with the changing population structure.

The "care provision maps" show how many elderly people there are per 100 people in the next younger generation who could theoretically help them, whether as relatives or as professional helpers. This ratio is already comparatively unfavourable in regions where the local economy is unable to provide sufficient employment for its population. In Germany, regions that are experiencing significant outward migration include the Harz and former inner-German border regions such as Lüchow-Dannenberg. In Switzerland similar tendencies can be observed in Schaffhausen and Appenzell. In some regions, an influx of older people may lead to a less favourable care potential ratio, but many of the pensioners who move, for example, to Garmisch-Partenkirchen or Baden-Baden are often sufficiently wealthy to afford private care services.

Within a space of 15 years, the ratio of very old people who may need care and the potential number of people who can help them will change dramatically. This ratio will be least favourable in the former industrial areas in West Germany, where employment opportunities have suffered following economic decline and the younger population has migrated elsewhere, as well as in the entire former East German region. By comparison, the population in Austria and Switzerland is comparatively young due to immigration from abroad, with the consequence that there will be a large number of potential carers.

Models for a respectful approach to dementia

The industrial nations, and Germany in particular, will be among the first countries to experience a development that the poorer nations are yet to see. As such they have a global responsibility to provide an example. Their societies must develop and test concepts for dealing with the challenge of dementia in a respectful manner.

First and foremost, those affected need to have a say. Important initiatives in this respect can be seen in Great Britain. Since 2002, the "Scottish Dementia Working Group" (SDWG), which is run exclusively by people with dementia, campaigns to improve services for people with dementia and to improve attitudes towards people with dementia. By actively lobbying local politics, they have managed to convince the Scottish government to take their needs seriously. For example, the Doctors and Health Care Staff Working Group have

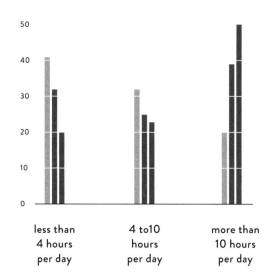

Degree of nursing care in hours in the different stages of dementia (data basis: Alzheimer Europe)

Degree of Dementia
light
medium
severe

improved awareness of the importance of early diagnosis to ensure a better quality of life for the person affected and their relatives. The SDWG activists employ unconventional methods of public relations including songs, comics and theatre projects.

It is not by chance that Great Britain is among those countries who have developed a national dementia policy, along with France, the Netherlands, Sweden, Norway and Australia. The governments of these countries have analysed the needs of people with dementia and their relatives as a basis for developing strategies for dealing with dementia. Concrete steps include, for example, better provision of information for the public, more opportunities for people with dementia to

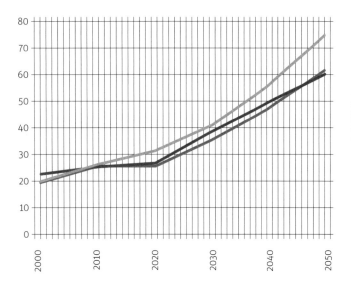

Number of over-79-year-olds per 100 persons aged between 50 and 64 from 2000 to 2050 in Germany, Austria and Switzerland

Germany
Austria
Switzerland

(data basis: Federal Statistical Office: 12th coordinated population projection Variant 1-W1, Austrian Conference on Spatial Planning: ÖROK Prognosis, Swiss Federal Statistical Office, own calculations)

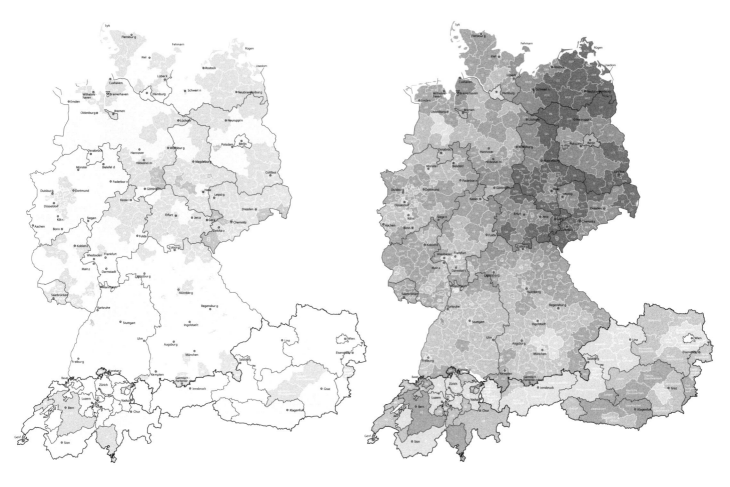

2008

2025

Map showing number of people with dementia per 10,000 residents by region in Germany, Austria, Switzerland and Liechtenstein, 2008 and 2025 (data basis: BBR Federal Office for Buildings and Regional Planning: Inkar 2009, Austrian Conference on Spatial Planning: ÖROK Prognoses, German Federal Statistical Office, Swiss Statistics, Statistics Austria, Statistical Office of the Principality of Liechtenstein, own calculations). The regional data on which the maps are based are available online: www.berlin-institute.org

less than 1.300
1.300 to 1.600
1.600 to 1.900
1.900 to 2.200
2.200 to 2.500
2.500 to 2.800
more than 2.800

participate in society, better provision of support and improved care provision. Furthermore, it is important that these ideas are adapted to the specific requirements of different regions and municipalities and are put into effect in cities as well as in rural areas.

France has, among other things, an exemplary system for integrating care provision. In many countries, dementia patients and their relatives must laboriously assemble the information and help they need from many different sources, and sometimes from commercial care providers and charitable organisations that are in competition with one another. In France, they need only consult a state-run "Local Information and Coordination Centre" (CLIC). With centres all over France, they represent a first port of call for all elderly people and their relatives. The staff can assist with everything from putting enquirers into contact with the right people to arranging a multi-disciplinary care assistance plan.

And there are also a series of model projects in which civil society organisations and the communities of local municipalities have themselves taken the initiative to improve the lives of people with dementia. In England, the Joseph Rowntree Foundation (JRF) has initiated large-scale projects in the cities of York and Bradford to help them become more liveable for people with dementia. In Germany, the City of Arnsberg has encouraged their citizens to contribute ideas for making the environment more friendly to the needs of people with dementia. They have documented their experiences in a handbook that aims to animate other municipalities to follow their example.

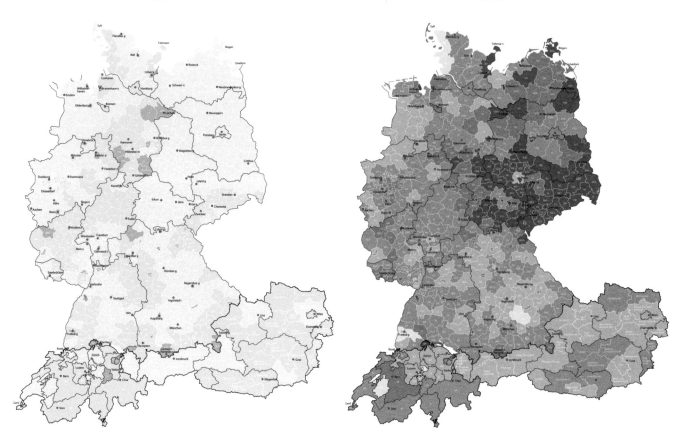

	2008		2025

Map showing number of over-79-year-olds per 100 persons aged between 50 and 64 by region in Germany, Austria, Switzerland and Liechtenstein, 2000 and 2025 (data basis: German Federal Statistical Office, Statistics Austria, Swiss Statistics, Statistical Office of the Principality of Liechtenstein, BBR Federal Office for Building and Regional Planning: Inkar 2009, Austrian Conference on Spatial Planning: ÖROK Prognoses, own calculations)

	less than 20
	21 to 26
	26 to 31
	31 to 36
	36 to 40
	41 and more

1 Alzheimer's Disease International, *World Alzheimer Report*. London 2009. www.alz.co.uk/research/files/WorldAlzheimerReport.pdf

2 Deutsche Stiftung Weltbevölkerung, *Datenreport*. Hanover 2012. www.slideshare.net/dicdsw/daten-report-2012

3 *Erster Altenbericht der Bundesregierung 1993*, Bundestagsdrucksache (Federal Parliament Paper) 12/5897; Ulman Lindenberger, Jacqui Smith, Karl-Ulrich Mayer and Paul B. Baltes (eds.), *Die Berliner Altersstudie*. Berlin 2010.

4 According to U. Ziegler and G. Doblhammer, "Prävalenz und Inzidenz von Demenz in Deutschland. Eine Studie auf Basis von Daten der gesetzlichen Krankenversicherungen von 2002" (Prevalence and Incidence of Dementia in Germany. A study based on data from the statutory health insurance providers from 2002). Rostocker Zentrum, discussion paper no. 24, 2009. www.rostockerzentrum.de

5 S. Menning and E. Hoffmann, "Die Babyboomer – ein demografisches Porträt", in: *GeroStat* 02/2009.

6 Deutsches Institut für Wirtschaftsforschung, Press release of 17 March 2010: "Renten im Osten rutschen unter die Grundsicherung". www.diw.de; M. Richter and K. Hurrelmann, "Gesundheit und soziale Ungleichheit", in: *Aus Politik und Zeitgeschichte* 42/2007.

7 Bundesministerium für Familie, Senioren, Frauen und Jugend (Federal Ministry of Family Affairs, Senior Citizens, Women and Youth), "Altern im Wandel. Zentrale Ergebnisse des Deutschen Alterssurveys". www.bmfsfj.de, 2010.

8 F. Beske et al., *Morbiditätsprognose 2050. Ausgewählte Krankheiten für Deutschland, Brandenburg und Schleswig-Holstein*. Fritz Beske Institut für Gesundheits-System-Forschung, Kiel 2009.

towards a dementia-friendly hospital

Gesine Marquardt

"How are we doing after the operation? Here's your breakfast!" George wakes with a start from his sleep. Who is the lady in the pink uniform, and what did she just say? And, where am I actually? Yellow walls ... perhaps a hotel? He tries to get up, but a plastic tube attached to his arm prevents him from doing so. He tugs at the tube and it comes off. In the background he can hear loud beeping. Shortly after, it stops and there is suddenly a man in the room who pushes a wheelchair towards Georg. "So, you weren't hungry then? Time to get you off to Echo over at level five!" George isn't sure if the man really expects him to sit in that wheelchair, but the man takes him by the arm and propels him into the chair and then out the door. They travel along corridors, turning off here and there. George isn't sure where they are going and why. Suddenly the wheelchair comes to a halt. The man behind him has gone too. Maybe he said something, but he's not sure. What should he do now? He gets up to have a look around. Not a soul. He starts off down the corridor. Suddenly a door opens automatically in front of him. Behind it, he can see a garden with trees. That looks like a nice place and off he goes.

For people with dementia, the closed, efficiency-optimised environment of a hospital is often so disorientating that the medical therapies they need fail to have the desired effect and the symptoms of dementia are exacerbated. Regardless of the respective medical field, hospitals are neither built nor staffed for the requirements and needs of people with dementia. Given that the proportion of over-65-year-olds now accounts for 43% of all hospital cases in Germany each year, and therefore that the number of patients requiring dementia-related treatment is rising, there is obviously a need for more dementia-friendly care programmes and an accordingly designed environment.

Numerous scientific studies have shown that architecture has the potential to benefit the process of recovery and to influence the behaviour and well-being of people with dementia. But although these findings are now being implemented around the world in the design and conversion of care homes for the elderly, hospitals are only just beginning to take such recommendations on board. In the search for suitable concepts, most new initiatives have until now been special units for people with dementia that are modelled on inpatient care homes for the elderly.

A possible model for future facilities are the "Acute Care for the Elderly" (ACE) units in the USA which aim to ensure

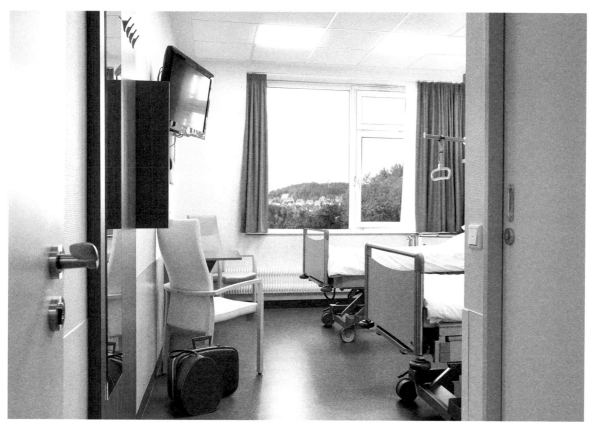

Geriatric Wing of the Maria-Hilf Hospital in Brilon, Germany. Interior design 100% interior, Sylvia Leydecker, 2013

that patients can remain as independent as possible during their stay in hospital. The combination of geriatric care by a multi-disciplinary professional team and a suitably designed living environment has proven to have a positive effect on the patients. A comparative study of patients at a usual care hospital unit showed that of the patients treated at ACE units fewer entered a care home directly after their treatment. In addition, there was less need for the use of restraints and medication and a lower mortality rate in the 12 months after release from the hospital. More importantly both patients as well as hospital administrators were highly satisfied with the ACE units. Specialised nursing areas for people with dementia are, however, not suitable for all patients and clinical symptoms, and the architectural design of hospitals as a whole needs to respond to the growing number of older patients. The following aspects are of particular importance:

Good orientation and ways of encouraging mobility
A central destination in the centre of the floor plan of a ward or unit, for example a common room, provides patients with a point of orientation and encourages them to be mobile. Similarly, the provision of a kitchen that patients can use to prepare simple meals or snacks means that patients need not

totally relinquish their everyday competences. The careful use of light, colour and materials can also be used to provide orientation: the use of contrast, for example, can be used to draw attention to areas that are relevant to patients and away from functional areas, which can be given a more monotonous colour treatment. Light is especially important in the patient rooms. Studies of care home patients reveal that most falls occur in the patient's own bedroom, and that many accidents occur on the way to or from the bathroom. As such it is important that it is sufficiently illuminated at night and that additional handholds are made available, for example in the form of a handrail.

Safety and security
The ongoing presence of staff at a central point in the ward or unit offers patients a sense of security and also helps to reduce the tendency among dementia patients to wander off. Some of the architectural means that are used in inpatient care facilities, such as the masking of exit doors by painting them in the same colour as the walls, are not so feasible in the interlinked corridors of hospitals. It is, however, possible to channel the movement of active patients by providing points of interests within the floor plan of a unit, for example an aquarium or seating niches at places where there is increased

Hospice of the Stiftung Marienhospital in Euskirchen, Germany. Interior design 100% interior, Sylvia Leydecker, 2011

activity. The clustering of a group of patient rooms within a ward along with a workplace for a member of staff also helps patients with dementia grasp their immediate environment and feel cared-for. For particularly anxious or unsettled patients as well as those who need to be monitored on an ongoing basis, the provision of semi-public zones with comfortable chairs or geriatric seats should be considered. When patients know that carers are close by, they are less anxious and therefore also more at ease.

Clear information cues

Patients spend much of their time alone in their room. Here they need to know where they are, the time of day, and perhaps also a time plan for the day. This can easily be achieved by providing a whiteboard or pinboard near the bed that details information such as the name and place of the hospital, the name of the on-duty nurse or carer as well as the time of any appointments that day. Making it possible for patients to have personal items at their bedside also helps reassure them where they are, although relatives are not always able to provide these when patients are only briefly in hospital.

Similarly, colour, light, symbols or numbers can be useful as a means of giving beds a distinctive appearance, in turn making them more recognisable for patients. The staff also needs to be able to tell at a glance what a patient's needs are (for example in the form of pictograms near the bed) and what aids, e.g. glasses or hearing, they use or may need.

All of the above are beneficial not only for patients with dementia, but also for all patients who find themselves in the unusual situation of being in a hospital. These elements provide an architecturally legible environment that gives patients a sense of orientation in time and place and where there is easy access to information. The result contributes not only to improving the care of a particular, albeit growing group of patients but also to making the architecture of the entire hospital more patient-friendly. And this in turn also serves as a basis for new marketing strategies. Many hospitals in industrial nations with ageing populations have started to advertise themselves as being "dementia-friendly". But competition is not the only motivator: hospitals are also under economic pressure to develop care concepts and architectural environments that improve the process of recovery along with the independence of the patients. Given the fact that patients are in hospital for ever shorter periods as a result of the Diagnosis Related Group (DRG) reimbursement system in Germany or the Medicare System in the USA, which define limits for the maximum number of treatment days, it is necessary to re-appraise how we address the needs of people with dementia. We need to find ways of reducing the acute sense of disorientation that being admitted to hospital creates. Likewise, hospitals need to be more strongly embedded in their urban and social context. To prevent "the revolving door effect" in which patients are repeatedly admitted to hospital, we also need better outpatient systems for pre- and post-treatment care. This could, for example, be undertaken by outreach care providers who are able to anticipate necessary treatment and can provide preparatory or preventive outpatient care. Telemedical solutions will also become more widespread in future and will in turn contribute to a reduction in hospital admissions, as will other forms of care for the elderly such as day care and low-level services such as daytime companionship that are emerging both in local neighbourhoods as well as in the care chain between the hospital institutions and living at home.

Distinctive design features aid orientation in long corridors. Conversion of a care home for the elderly, Stavangerstraße 26, Berlin, Germany. Feddersen Architekten, 2004

Spacious, light-filled corridor. Elias Hospice in St. Marien Hospital in Ludwigshafen, Germany. sander.hofrichter architekten, 2005

Ample space to walk about and look around without losing one's orientation.
Centre for Mental Health, Neuss, Germany. sander.hofrichter architekten, 2012

A change of perspective. Old and new connected by the entrance hall of the Centre for Mental Health, Neuss, Germany. sander.hofrichter architekten, 2012

finding home
in central station

Uwe Rada

1

Where have they gone? They were here last time. *Ditsch?*
Wiener Feinbäckerei, Le Crobag? One of these bakers had
butter pretzels on offer, I'm sure. I love butter pretzels. I was
born in South Germany, in butter pretzel land so to speak.
They remind me of home. And home is where I know my way
around. I head off in search of a piece of home in the Hauptbahnhof (central station) and cannot find it.

2

I can remember the first time I visited the Hauptbahnhof very
clearly. I think it was a day or two after it had opened. Berlin
made a big thing about the architecture with a grand opening
ceremony, but I was more interested in the practical aspects.
Would the Hauptbahnhof make my journeys any shorter?

I came with a bird's-eye view in my head. Berlin used to have
Bahnhof Zoo and the *Ostbahnhof* – which in those days used
to be called Hauptbahnhof, when we still had the GDR.
Before then, in the times of Emperor Wilhelm and the Weimar
Republic, Berlin used to be proud of its end of line "Kopfbahn-
höfe". Kopf: head; Bahnhof: railway station. What a combination! A railway station in one's head? I guess you only go one
way from there: out of one's head. It doesn't get any more
practical than that.

But now we're in the 21st century – and today the station is an
InterCity Express Junction. Kind of makes sense too when you
look at it from above. Only one thing had me puzzled on my
first visit. Why do all the ICE trains only go south and west,
to Leipzig and Munich or Hamburg and Hanover? Why not also
northwards to Stralsund, Szczecin or Warsaw?

3

So much for the InterCity Express Junction: more of an idea
than reality. I wasn't really getting anywhere with the bird's-
eye view, so I decided to switch to a worm's-eye perspective.
From here the Hauptbahnhof looks less like a junction
than a labyrinth with different levels, escalators, glass lifts.
It reminded me of those illusionary drawings by M.C. Escher.
I would have to take things slowly. To begin with, I decided to
get two things clear in my mind: my train to Stuttgart leaves
from the overground platform – Hauptbahnhof (hoch) – and
the trains to Leipzig or Hamburg from the underground platforms – Hauptbahnhof (tief).

4

I always come by S-Bahn. And I always change at Friedrich-
strasse and then get into one of the carriages at the front.
In the Hauptbahnhof, I always use the escalator from Platform
16, the one with the blue and white advert for the *AO-Hostel*

175,000 square metres gross floor area is spread over five levels.

Excessive visual stimuli and a lack of clear points of reference in the building's architecture hamper orientation.

Daylight spills into the building, creating a pleasant atmosphere that reaches right into the depths of the building.

Numerous escalators and lifts facilitate direct barrier-free access to and transfer between the different platforms.

am Zoo that looks a little like the *Hertha* Football Club's colours from afar. Opposite, on the other side, you can see *Ditsch*, the *Wiener Feinbäckerei* and *Le Crobag*. I think so, anyway. Perhaps that's one level further down? In train stations – in the big ones anyway – it's a lot like in life. You're taking a risk if you leave the trodden path.

5

If you take a look at the architects' plans, there's no risk, only numbers and certainty. "The Hauptbahnhof in Berlin, built between 1996 and 2006, contains a gross floor area of 175,000 square metres and has five levels." That's what it says on the homepage of von Gerkan, Marg and Partner. I like the homepage, because it also mentions the bird's-eye view: "This is where the new underground north-south ICE rail link crosses the arcing course of the west-east train lines. Two S-Bahn lines come from both directions and there is a U-Bahn line connecting north and south. The north-south route is located 15 metres below ground in a tunnel that passes beneath the River Spree and the entire Tiergarten. Here there is an underground railway station with eight mainline tracks and four platforms for mainline and regional trains."

I'm not sure that helps me much. Can anyone on Platform 16 tell me which direction is north, which is east, south or west? How are you supposed to know which direction you're facing when all around is empty wasteland?

6

The architects don't say anything about the *Europaplatz* or *Washingtonplatz* on their website. I always forget which end of the station is the *Washingtonplatz* and which is the *Europaplatz*. It's not that this doesn't matter. Berlin is in Europe, so the Hauptbahnhof should be at home on the *Europaplatz*. Why can't I memorise that? I only know that one of the two squares faces the River Spree while the other faces into the city. But soon you won't be able to see the Spree anyway when they build all those hotels and offices between the station and the Spree, blocking the view. Maybe, when they're done, I'll have a coffee in one of those blocks. Then I'll know which end is which. *Washingtonplatz* or *Europaplatz*? I guess the reason I get confused is because I don't often leave the station on foot. I come by train and leave by train.

7

Once I came to the station, not as a traveller but by car. I had to pick up a visitor. My visitor said I had to come because he wouldn't be able to find his way around such a large station. I was to come as his navigator. And I came by car because my visitor had lots of luggage. When I left the car park, got into the elevator and pressed "Hauptbahnhof (tief)", I thought I'd lost my way. The lift went down! My car wasn't parked below the railway station after all but above me. When you're in the belly of the station, neither the bird's-eye view nor the worm's-eye perspective are much help. I guess the innards of the Hauptbahnhof have a life of their own. Like the Paris Opera House in that famous phantom novel.

The train with my visitor is late. It's cold on platform 1. There's a draught and it's still. A bit like when I go down into the cellar at home, the dark corner of our block of flats. "You'll soon be back upstairs," I say to myself. But on platform 1, I have to wait. The escalator purrs almost silently. Nobody there to keep me company. I wish I had a butter pretzel with me. That would be nice.

I start to panic. When my visitor arrives and we get him safely stowed in the car, will I be able to find my way back out of the belly of the station? Will I make it back to Berlin with all its streets, full of traffic jams but devoid of activities that take possession of urban space? What I'd really like is, when I'm back at the top, to descend the stairs that lead to the Humboldthafen. That's the end of the line. Unless, that is, a vaporetto were to pull up at the Humboldthafen.

8

Paul Virilio, that theorist of the fleeting, once wrote that airports and train stations are the cities of the future. I find it hard to believe him. In the city where I live, I know where to get butter pretzels – where you can always get them. That's why I feel at home in this city. At the Hauptbahnhof, I don't feel at home. Be that as it may, I've solved the mystery of the butter pretzels: I went back a few days later and they were there again: in the *Wiener Feinbäckerei*. "I couldn't find any the other day," I asked the man behind the counter, "What happened?" His answer was a relief. I hadn't lost my senses after all. "The butter pretzels?" he said, "Oh, they were sold out."

Note: Margherita Lazzati uses photography to tell complex narratives. Her series on Berlin central station was taken in 2013. The photographer lives and works in Milan, Italy. Her photos have appeared in numerous exhibitions in Italy and abroad.

land custom station

Agartala, India

Architects
Anagram Architects

Client
The State Government of Tripura, India

Completion
under construction

Gross floor area
9,452 m²

The Land Custom Station (LCS) at the India-Bangladesh Border at Agartala is a large facility providing transit, customs and immigration and cargo handling services for goods and passengers travelling between Bangladesh and Northeast India. The central architectural concept for the proposed LCS centers on the idea of the "Portal". The LCS is truly the Gateway for entering or leaving Indian Territory. The design intends to convey this concept very strongly. The LCS is also a bridge between neighbouring nations. It is vital for the architecture of the LCS to reflect the shared linkages of the nation with its neighbour. In order to achieve this in a contextual manner, the design draws strongly from the local expertise in bamboo as manifested in the intricately crafted gateways set into the fences of Agartala.

Bamboo, in its multiple forms, is a deeply significant cultural anchor for people on both sides of the border. Inspired by the ubiquitous gateways and fences of the region, the design reinterprets their traditional sophistication in bamboo craft in a modular steel-bamboo construction.

The architects believed that if the use of bamboo could be successfully married to an existing structure then it would demonstrate its relevance today in a more convincing way. Therefore it was decided to retain the structure and reuse it. The design develops modular steel bamboo structures in which the bamboo members may be replaced without disturbing the functioning of the LCS. Steel is used as brackets and rigid (compressive) members whereas bamboo is used for its tensile properties in covering large spans. This is used to create fences and roofing structures.

The roof structure of the Passenger Holding Facility interprets the form of the traditional Tripuri gabled roof with skylights. The materials used for roofing are modern and permanent with excellent weather-proof detailing employed in their fixing and installation.

The plinths of all the new construction are raised to up to one metre with pronounced plinth protection. The building volumes are punctuated by the use of large fenestrations and deep verandahs. These elements add to the light and minimal articulation of the edifices.

Border outpost with traditional Tripuri gable roofs

View of the border outpost with the 8-metre-high bamboo enclosure in the background

View of the terminal for cross-border trade and passengers. The surrounding outdoor areas are covered by a steel and bamboo roof construction.

lingang new city

Lingang, China

Competition
2002/2003 –
1st prize

Design
gmp Architekten
von Gerkan, Marg
und Partner

Client
Shanghai Harbour
City Development
(Group) Co., Ltd.

Partner
Nikolaus Goetze

Port planning
HPC Hamburg Port
Consulting

Landscape architects
Breimann & Bruun

Light planning
Schlotfeldt Licht

Inhabitants
800,000

Construction period
2003–2020

Area
74,000 m²

Lingang New City – a newly planned city for 800,000 inhabitants that will be completed by 2020 – is situated approximately 70 km southeast of Shanghai between the mouths of the Yangtze and Qiantang Rivers. Construction of the city, which is conceived as a separate harbour city, began in 2003 according to plans by the Hamburg-based architecture office of gmp – von Gerkan, Marg und Partner. Its design represents a departure from both the ideals of other newly planned cities from the last century, such as Brasilia, Canberra and Chandigarh, as well as the historically evolved urban grain of the European city of the 19th century. In its centre lies a circular 2.5-kilometre-wide artificial lake. The master plan draws on the metaphor of concentric ripples formed by a drop falling into water: the lake in the centre is surrounded by an eight-kilometre-long lakeside promenade with a bathing beach à la Copacabana, which in turn is adjoined by a car-free business district with offices, shops and high-density residential buildings. The next ring is a circular urban park with a number of solitary public buildings, and beyond that a series of residential neighbourhoods for 13,000 inhabitants each.

More than two million trees have already been planted in Lingang as part of intensive greening measures aimed at creating a pleasant local climate and quality of life. In addition, waterways and small lakes can be found throughout the city, reinforcing the atmosphere of "waterside living". But the main attraction of the city is without doubt "Lake Dishui" at the heart of the circular city which accommodates a diverse range of recreational activities. In marked contrast to most inner cities in China, and indeed around the world, the centre is not beset by smog and traffic jams, but instead serves as a peaceful core area with recreational facilities that provide a good quality of life for all its residents. For Meinhard von Gerkan and his team of planners the only disappointment was the inability to fully realise the originally envisaged arrangement of blocks and courtyards, intended to encourage neighbourly communication, because the rigid principles of Feng Shui prescribe that all residential blocks must be oriented in an east-west direction.

The new lake with its beach and promenade as well as the high proportion of open, public spaces have made Lingang one of the largest and most attractive tourist destinations and local recreation areas in China. Nevertheless, despite its clear attractions and the promise of its marketing campaign – "Lingang. Better City, Better Life" –, the city planning authorities still make sure that sufficient affordable housing continues to be built to ensure a social mix.

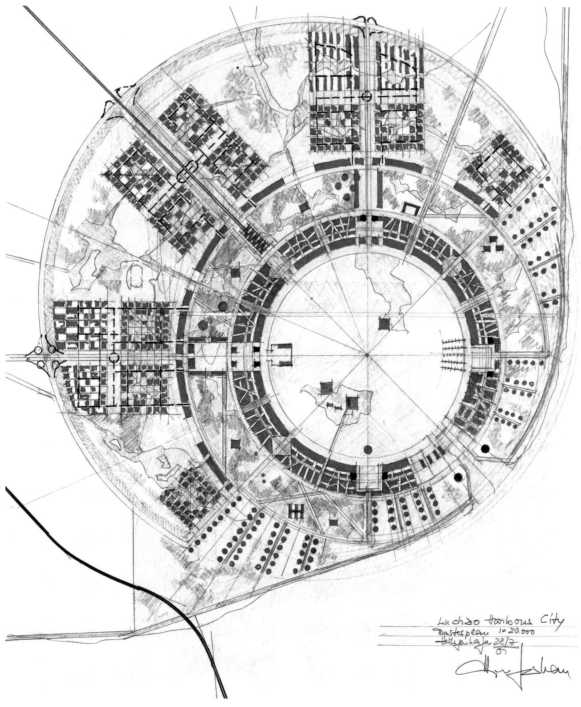

Design sketch for Luchao Harbour City in 2001, which later became Lingang New City, China

Photo of the model showing the radial pattern of rings and functions

Urban park with freestanding buildings

Landmarks such as the Maritime Museum with its expressive roof shape provide orientation and identification.

cittaslow –
stopping places in a
fast-moving world

Cittaslow is Italian for "slow town" and characterises small communities that offer pleasant environments with a good quality of life in which to grow old. The movement began in four small towns in Italy in 1999 and has since spread around the world and now enjoys an international following. More than 100 communities have joined the global network and committed to fostering their historical legacy, traditions, environment and sustainability as a counterpoint to the increasing uniformity of today's fast-paced world. A focus on healthy food and regional produce as well as the safeguarding of local employment and better historical awareness are some of the aspects that aim to improve the quality of life. The potential that this concept can offer for promoting the social inclusion of people with dementia is a topic for further investigation.

The Opelvillen Rüsselsheim Art and Culture Foundation (photo on the right) puts on similar initiatives: on non-public days, the exhibition centre opens to allow people with dementia to undertake accompanied visits to the gallery. The opportunity to look at art is not only pleasurable but also stimulating and encourages communication.

dementia, local municipalities and public space

Insights and perspectives

Peter Wißmann

In the year 2007, *Aktion Demenz*, a civil society organisation working at a national level launched a public campaign for "dementia-friendly municipalities". The initiative argued that living with dementia, while much discussed in conferences, actually takes place "on the ground" in our everyday social realm. Without negating the relevance of the meta level (legislation, care provision infrastructure etc.), the micro level also plays a vital role in the experience of day-to-day activities and quality of life as well as in ensuring that people can still take part in society. As a consequence, municipalities should also be seen as a potential vehicle for bringing about change. The term "dementia-friendly municipality" is neither a clearly defined concept nor is it merely a label. Rather, it aims to express a vision for coordinating actions and is based on a series of fundamental considerations and essential ideas,[1] in particular that dementia must be seen as a social issue for society as a whole, and that people with dementia should also be able to participate in and interact with the public realm just like anyone else.

A space of appearance for us as individuals
In her writings, Hannah Arendt accords public space central importance as the place in which we conduct our daily affairs and in which we negotiate how we live with one another. It is a space of appearance for each of us as individuals and it is by entering this space that we express our freedom to transcend our own lives and to step into our common world.[2]

It is where people meet one another and experience themselves as an active member of society. As such, it must be possible for every one of us to have access to the public realm. In the context, or the vision, of dementia-friendly municipalities this means that we must overcome the prevailing forms of care that segregate the ill and infirm into parallel worlds (for example nursing homes and so-called dementia neighbourhoods). Dementia-friendly communities need instead to find inclusive housing and care concepts and strategies that enable participation in social space. In this context, the term "inclusion" means that it is possible for people who are affected by dementia and those who are not to interact and be together in public space and that those suffering from dementia are able to articulate their own needs and take part in social life. The UN Convention on the Rights of Persons with Disabilities states this as a basic prerequisite, but even municipalities that have set themselves the aim to become dementia-friendly communities are as yet far from having realised the ideal of inclusion.

"Outdoors" as public space
From an urban design and sociological viewpoint, public space – described as a place with special qualities that is intensively used and caters for a wide range of social activities – is also seen as a space that is accessible at any time and without restrictions for all residents of a community, such as a city.[3] Here too, we need to examine the degree with which people with cognitive impairments are able to move around freely in public

The ability to use the public realm and participate in communal activities is an important factor for one's quality of life.

space or are prevented from using it. The culture and media scientist Gabriele Kreutzner emphasises how important the outdoor environment and its usability is for the quality of life of people with dementia and their ability to participate in daily life.[4] She cites findings that show that modern cities exclude specific social groups (including people with disabilities) from taking part in social life due to their design and historical form, and presents the results of studies on the accessibility of urban environments for people with cognitive impairments. These studies also describe how the careful design of outdoor environments can help people with dementia to orientate and find their way. Up to now, however, very few of these findings have been put into practice.

The small town of Ostfildern near Stuttgart in southwest Germany is a good example of a local initiative to establish a "dementia-friendly municipality". Over a period of nine months in 2007–2008, the initiative undertook a dementia awareness campaign entitled "We are neighbours" that later served as a model for numerous other initiatives elsewhere in Germany. Focussing on awareness-raising events (information, culture), regular intensive public relations activities and guidance for police officers, local businesses and members of associations, the campaign was part of a long-term general strategy aimed at establishing dementia-friendly structures. In response to the awareness-raising events, opportunities were created for people with and without dementia to

come together, for example, in the form of musical request programmes or church services. In place of a care home, the municipality set up a neighbourhood centre that in addition to hosting social and cultural activities (local citizens' meetings, open art workshop etc.) also offers a range of housing and care concepts: shared housing for people with dementia with outpatient care, communal households with live-in carers, a day care centre as well as apartments for the disabled. A key aim was to establish links with the local community, enabling people with and without dementia to communicate – in short to promote inclusion and participation. The activities in the open art workshop and the local citizens' meetings have been particularly successful in this regard and all of the initiatives in Ostfildern can now count on a well-developed local network of support from local residents and the backing of local politics. A website was set up to document the dementia awareness campaign and provides information on ongoing activities: www.demenz-ostfildern.de.

Arnsberg in the German state of North Rhine-Westphalia is another example of a local municipality that has actively sought to tackle the challenges of demographic change. The city embarked on a process of consultation with older citizens of the city with a view to finding ways to make the city more suitable for its ageing residents while maintaining its active, vibrant and cosmopolitan outlook. These deliberations were later expanded to include ways of making the community more dementia-friendly. With the help of funding from the Robert Bosch Foundation, Arnsberg became a "learning workshop", a city that aims to benefit other municipalities by sharing what it has learned. Key aspects included better co-ordination between professional services and local initiatives as well as intergenerational events ("a multi-generational circus") and the creation of networks. A specialist unit entitled "Zukunft im Alter" (A Future for the Elderly) was set up that initiates, monitors and coordinates these activities.[5]

Dementia-friendly municipalities and the outdoor realm

While not the only important aspect, the design of the outdoor environment and its (non-)accessibility for people with cognitive impairments is certainly a key element of a dementia-friendly community. Now that several years have passed since the dementia-friendly municipalities campaign began, what practical meaning has this acquired in the everyday work of the regional initiatives and projects? At present, this is hard to answer as, with a few notable exceptions,[6] very few evaluation reports have been published, and those that are available typically document individual initiatives. An evaluation conducted as part of the second phase of the "People with Dementia in the Municipality" programme funded by the Robert Bosch Foundation also has a rather limited scope.[7] Twelve case study projects were visited and group interviews were conducted on site with the project participants. The evaluation describes aspects such as "civil society profile" or "relevance of citizens' participation in the project work" but reveals little about the design of the outdoor environment and how it is used by people with dementia. Despite the lack of empirical findings, the author concludes that this aspect has not played a significant role in the current dementia-friendly municipality projects.

Conclusions

A concept of "dementia-friendliness" that is founded on knowledge, awareness and acceptability aspects alone and does not encompass "robust" structural factors such as accessible outdoor environments and the ability for people with cognitive impairments to use public space (to articulate themselves and to meet, exchange and take part with others) fails to provide local municipalities with the strategic plans of actions that they need. As a consequence, the existing awareness-building initiatives urgently need to be taken a step further to include the aforementioned points. This means actively seeking the opinions of professionals from other disciplines such as urban planners and architects. Above all, however, it means including the true experts in the field – people with dementia – in the development of corresponding activities and strategies.

1 See also: P. Wißmann and R. Gronemeyer, *Demenz und Zivilge-sellschaft – Eine Streitschrift*. Frankfurt am Main 2008, pp. 73–77; and R. Gronemeyer and P. Wißmann: "Was demenziell Erkrankte brauchen – Auf dem Weg zu einer demenzfreundlichen Kommune", in Bertelsmann-Stiftung (ed.), *Initiieren – planen – umsetzen. Handbuch kommunale Seniorenpolitik*. Gütersloh 2009, pp. 211–213.

2 Cited in M. Stauch, *Hannah Arendts Konzeption des Gemeinsinns im Hinblick auf den Kommunitarismus. Politisches Handeln in nachmetaphysischer Zeit*, 2005. www.math.hu-berlin.de/~stauch/Hannah_Arendt.pdf

3 S. Reiß-Schmidt, *Der öffentliche Raum. Traum, Wirklichkeit, Perspektiven*. www.urbanauten.de/reiss_schmidt.pdf

4 G. Kreutzner, "Die Entdeckung des (Dr-)Außen: Die äußere Umgebung als Faktor der Lebensqualität von Menschen mit Demenz", in: *DeSS-orientiert*.

5 Arnsberg's experience as a "learning workshop" has been documented in a publication available online: *Arnsberg "Lern-Werkstadt" Demenz. Handbuch für Kommunen*. Arnsberg 2011. www.projekt-demenz-arnsberg.de

6 See for example: Demenz Support Stuttgart, Esslingen University of Applied Sciences, *Evaluation der Demenzkampagne Ostfildern. Wir sind Nachbarn*, 2009, project report. www.demenz-ostfildern.de

7 C. Jurk, *Aktion Demenz e.V.: Menschen mit Demenz in der Kommune*, Evaluation of 12 practice projects in the second project phase 2012.

People with and without dementia taking part in a church service

About the authors

SUSAN BLACK, born in Montreal, Canada, received her Master's degree in architecture from the University of Manitoba. She is a founding partner of Perkins Eastman Black Architects in Toronto, Canada. Healthcare has been a major focus in her firm, creating new approaches for acute and complex continuing care, dementia and children-friendly environments, and ambulatory facilities globally.

Prof. Dr. GABRIELE BRANDSTETTER completed her doctorate on Clemens Brentano at the University of Munich and her habilitation on *Tanz-Lektüren. Körperbilder und Raumfiguren der Avantgarde* (1995; second expanded edition 2013). She is Professor of Theatre and Dance Studies at the Freie Universität Berlin. Most recently she has published *Dance (and) Theory* (2013, co-edited with Gabriele Klein) and *Aging Body in Dance* (2014).

ECKHARD FEDDERSEN, born in Husum, Germany, in 1947, studied architecture (Karlsruhe, USA, Berlin) and worked at the Faculty of Architecture at the TU Berlin before founding his first office in 1973 together with Wolfgang von Herder. He was planning director of the Berlin Building Exhibition in 1999 and founded Feddersen Architekten in 2002. Together with Insa Lüdtke he has published *Living for the Elderly: A Design Manual*. Alongside his work as an architect, he is a speaker, expert assessor and journalist.

Dr. RALPH FISCHER is a scholar of theatre and culture. He studied theatre studies in Mainz, Vienna, Berlin and New York and completed his doctorate on *Walking Artists. Gehen in den performativen Künsten*. In 2010 he became director of cultural studies at the Evangelische Akademie in Frankfurt am Main. Ralph Fischer is the author of numerous publications in the fields of performance theory, theatre and cultural studies.

JONATHAN FRANZEN, born in 1959, is an American novelist. His third novel, *The Corrections*, earned Franzen the National Book Award and was a finalist for the Pulitzer Prize. In 2002, Franzen published a collection of essays entitled *How to Be Alone* and his fourth novel, *Freedom*, was published in 2010. A recurring theme of Franzen's writing is the disintegration of the family and how the fates of individuals relate to the wider social and political developments around them.

BENTE HEINIG, born in Berlin, Germany, in 1980, first studied law at the Freie Universität Berlin before studying medicine in Greifswald. She presently works at the Metabolic Centre of the Charité university hospital in Berlin and is a project doctor in the Berlin Aging Study II.

ANN HEYLIGHEN, born in Leuven, Belgium, in 1973, studied architecture and engineering in Leuven and Zurich. After receiving her PhD from KU Leuven she conducted postdoctoral research at Harvard University and UC Berkeley. She is a professor at KU Leuven and a member of the Research[x] Design group at the same institution.

Dr. DIETER HOFFMANN-AXTHELM, born in Berlin, Germany, in 1940, studied theology, philosophy and history. Today he works as a journalist and urban planner in Berlin.

CHRISTEL KAPITZKI, born in Duisburg, Germany, in 1959, studied literature and history of art at the Freie Universität Berlin. As a journalist and freelance author, she has published books and films on the topics of architecture, design and dance since 1991.

ELENI KOLOVOU (MAA, Dipl. Eng. Architect at University of Patras and UPC, Barcelona), born in Athens, Greece, works as an architect as well as a game designer/educator of location based mobile games with published work on both fields. Her current research focuses on parametric design and hybrid urban experience.

Prof. Dr. Dr. h.c. ANDREAS KRUSE became Director of the Institute of Gerontology at Heidelberg University in 1997. He studied psychology, philosophy, psychopathology and music. He has won a number of national and international scientific awards including an honorary doctorate from Osnabrück University.

INSA LÜDTKE, born in Tübingen, Germany, in 1972, began working as a freelance journalist in the fields of architecture, housing and health care in 2000 after completing her architectural studies at the TU Darmstadt. In 2008 she founded Cocon Concept, offering consulting and studies for the social, property and health care sectors. She is a frequent speaker, mediator and workshop leader and is the author of numerous publications.

Prof. Dr.-Ing. h.c. Dipl.-Ing. VOLKWIN MARG, born in Königsberg in East Prussia in 1936 is an architect and founding partner of the architecture office von Gerkan, Marg und Partner together with Meinhard von Gerkan. His office has realised over 350 buildings around the world. He is a member of the German Academy for Urban Design and Regional Planning, a member of the Free Academy of the Arts in Hamburg and in Berlin and recipient of numerous awards. He lectures and publishes widely.

Dr.-Ing. GESINE MARQUARDT, born in Dresden, Germany, in 1974, studied architecture at the University of Stuttgart and the New York Institute of Technology. She completed her doctorate on the dementia-friendly design of care facilities for the elderly and currently directs a research group at the TU Dresden on architecture in the context of demographic change.

DAVID McNAIR BA, CEng., FILP, born in Scotland, UK, in 1955. A lighting specialist and past president of the Institution of Lighting Professionals he works with the University of Stirling to develop knowledge on the benefits of light and lighting for older people, particularly those with dementia.

Dr. DOROTHEA MUTHESIUS, born in 1958, studied music, music therapy and sociology in Berlin. She works as a music therapist in residential groups for people with dementia and develops and evaluates practice projects in the field of the care of old people. She completed her doctorate on the function of music in personal biographies and lectures in courses on care for the elderly and music therapy in the master's study programme on music therapy at the Universität der Künste Berlin and University of Applied Sciences Würzburg-Schweinfurt. Most recently she published Muthesius et al. (2010): *Musik–Demenz–Begegnung. Musiktherapie für Menschen mit Demenz.*

Prof. Dr. WOLF D. OSWALD, born in Nuremberg, Germany, in 1940, is founding director of the Institute of Psychogerontology at the Friedrich-Alexander-Universität in Erlangen-Nuremberg. In 2006 he became head of the Research Group for Prevention and Dementia and is a founding partner of the SimA Academy. He is the author of over 250 publications.

ANNETTE POLLOCK, born in Windsor, UK, in 1946, studied architecture and landscape architecture at the University of Edinburgh. She is Director of Landscape Design at the University of Stirling's Dementia Services Development Centre (DSDC). With Mary Marshall, she co-edited the book *The Design of Outdoor Spaces for People with Dementia,* published in 2012.

RICHARD POLLOCK, born in Scotland, UK, in 1946, studied architecture, urban design and regional planning as well as philosophy in Edinburgh. In 1974, he set up the architecture practice Burnett Pollock Associates (now BPA-Architecture), specialising in design for disabilities. In 1993, he was appointed an associate architect with the then newly formed Dementia Services Development Centre at the University of Stirling and became their director of architecture in 2008. Richard is a speaker on the international stage and an author and contributor to numerous books about design for disabilities and dementia.

UWE RADA, born in Göppingen, Germany, in 1963, studied history and German literature at the Freie Universität Berlin. He is subject editor for urban development at the German daily newspaper *taz.* Rada has written several books, most recently *Die Elbe. Europas Geschichte im Fluss.* He lives in Berlin. www.uwe-rada.de

MICHAEL SCHMIEDER, born in Germany in 1955, is a trained nurse with additional training in emergency care. In 1980 he moved to Switzerland and became director of Sonnweid in 1985 where he develops concepts for the inpatient care of people with dementia, such as the concept of care oases. In 2001 he undertook a Master's degree in applied ethics at the University of Zurich. He is a sought-after speaker and consultant in the field of inpatient care forms in the treatment of dementia and has written numerous articles in the trade press.

Prof. Dr. med. ELISABETH STEINHAGEN-THIESSEN, born in Flensburg, Germany, in 1946, studied medicine in Marburg. Today she heads the chair for Gerontology and Nutrition Science at the Charité university hospital in Berlin. She is a member of the German Ethics Council and heads a series of interdisciplinary research projects, including the Berlin Aging Study II.

SABINE SÜTTERLIN, born in Scherzingen, Switzerland, in 1956, studied biochemistry and cell biology at the ETH Zurich. As a freelance science author, she has written many books including the *Demenz Report* published in 2011 by the Berlin Institute for Population and Development.

BETH TAUKE is Associate Professor of Architecture and Associate Dean at the State University of New York at Buffalo. She is project director at the center for Inclusive Design and Environmental Access (IDeA), a leading research centre on inclusive design in the U.S. Tauke's research and publications focus on multisensory perception, particularly as it relates to gestalt principles.

FRIEDERIKE TEBBE studied philosophy and fine art at the Ludwig-Maximilians-Universität in Munich and the Academy of Fine Arts, also in Munich. Thereafter she worked as a lecturer on colour and design at the UdK in Berlin. In 2001 she founded studio farbarchiv for her artistic work where she develops colour concepts for architects, businesses and private clients. Her work has been published in the book *Farbräume – Color Spaces.*

CHANTAL VAN AUDENHOVE, born in Gent, Belgium, in 1956, holds a doctoral degree in clinical psychology. She is a professor at KU Leuven and director of the LUCAS Centre for Care Research and Consultancy.

She also works as a coordinator for the Policy Research Centre on Welfare, Public Health and Family.

IRIS VAN STEENWINKEL, born in Saintes, France, in 1986, studied architecture and engineering at the Department of Architecture, Urbanism and Planning at KU Leuven, where she is currently pursuing a PhD in the Research[x]Design group, focussing on the spatial experiences of people with dementia.

Dipl. Psych. MONIKA WACHTER, born in Neustadt an der Aisch, Germany, in 1966, studied psychology at the Friedrich-Alexander-Universität (FAU) in Erlangen-Nuremberg. In 2008 she joined the Research Group for Prevention and Dementia at the Institute of Psychogerontology at FAU.

PETER WISSMANN, born in Dinslaken, Germany, in 1956, studied social pedagogy and social work at the University of Social Work in Berlin (now Alice Solomon University of Applied Sciences). He is managing director and scientific director of the Demenz Support Stuttgart gGmbH, publisher of the magazine *demenz. DAS MAGAZIN* and author of numerous publications.

MARKUS ZENS, born in Erding, Germany, in 1977, studied geography at the Friedrich-Alexander-Universität in Erlangen-Nuremberg, the Freie Universität Berlin and Al-Neelain University in Khartoum, Sudan. He is head of public relations at the EGZB Geriatric Centre in Berlin.

Reference literature

Arch+ No. 176/177, *Wohnen – wer mit wem, wo, wie, warum*, Aachen, 2006

Bachelard, G.: *The Poetics of Space*, Boston: Beacon Press, 1994

Baier, F. X.: *Der Raum, Prolegomena zu einer Architektur des gelebten Raumes*, Cologne: Verlag der Buchhandlung Walther König, 2000

Bickel, H.: *Die Epidemiologie der Demenz*, information sheet, Deutsche Alzheimer Gesellschaft e. V. Selbsthilfe Demenz, Berlin, 2012

Blume, T.; Duhm, B.: *Bauhaus. Bühne. Dessau*, Berlin: Jovis Verlag, 2008

Bollnow, F. O.: *Mensch und Raum*, Stuttgart: Kohlhammer, 1963

Brawley, E. C.: *Design Innovations for Aging and Alzheimer's. Creating Caring Environments.* Hoboken, New Jersey: Wiley, 2006

Cantley, C. and Wilson, R. C.: *Put Yourself in my Place. Designing and Managing Care Homes for People with Dementia*, Bristol: The Policy Press, 2002

Cohen, U. and Weisman, G. D.: *Holding on to Home. Designing Environments for People with Dementia*, Baltimore: Johns Hopkins University Press, 1991

Deutscher Ethikrat (ed.): *Demenz – Ende der Selbstbestimmung?* Vorträge der Tagung des Deutschen Ethikrates 2010, Berlin: Deutscher Ethikrat, 2012

Feddersen, E. and Lüdtke, I. (eds.): *Living for the Elderly*, Basel, Berlin, Boston: Birkhäuser, 2009

Galfetti, G. G.: *My House, My Paradise. The Construction of the Ideal Domestic Universe*, Barcelona: Gustavo Gili, 1999

Heeg, S. and Bäuerle, K.: *Heimat für Menschen mit Demen, Aktuelle Entwicklungen in Pflegeheimen*, Frankfurt am Main: Mabuse, 2008

Kämmer, K.: *50 Tipps für die Umsetzung von mehr Lebensqualität bei Menschen mit Demenz*, Hanover: Schlütersche, 2013

Karrer, D.: *Der Umgang mit dementen Angehörigen. Über den Einfluss sozialer Unterschiede*, Wiesbaden: VS Verlag für Sozialwissenschaften, 2009

Krämer, K. H. (ed.): *Building for the Elderly* (Architektur + Wettbewerbe, no. 212), Stuttgart: Krämer, 2007

Kruse, A.: *Lebensqualität bei Demenz? Zum gesellschaftlichen und individuellen Umgang mit einer Grenzsituation im Alter*, Heidelberg: Akademische Verlagsgesellschaft AKA, 2010

Living. Frontiers of Architecture III-IV (exhibition catalogue), Humblebaek Louisiana Museum of Modern Art, 2011

Marquardt, G.: *Kriterienkatalog demenzfreundlicher Architektur*, Berlin: Logos Verlag, 2007

Marshall, M. and Pollock, A. (eds.): *Designing Outdoor Spaces for People with Dementia*, Greenwich, N. S. W.: Hammond Press, 2012

Mühlegg-Weibel, A. (ed.): *Demenz verstehen. Leitfaden für die Praxis*, Wetzikon: Sonnweid AG, 2011

Payk, T. R.: *Demenz*, Munich: Reinhardt, 2010

Rau, U. (ed.): *Barrierefrei – Bauen für die Zukunft*, Berlin: Beuth Verlag, 2013 (3rd ed.)

Riley, T.: "The Un-Private House", in: *The Un-Private House* (exhibition catalogue), New York, NY: MoMA, 1999

Robert-Bosch-Stiftung (ed.): *Gemeinsam für ein besseres Leben mit Demenz*, Berne: Huber, 2007

Ronnberg, A. and Martin, K. (eds): *The Book of Symbols. Reflections on Archetypal Images*, Cologne: Taschen, 2011

Schaal, H. D.: *Innenräume – Interior Spaces*, Berlin: Ernst & Sohn, 1995

Utton, D.: *Designing Homes for People with Dementia*, London: The Journal of Dementia Care, Hawker Publications, 2007

Waldherr, G.: "Ruhe bewahren. Tradition, Heimat, Werte. Das klingt muffig und reaktionär. Doch es kann auch ganz modern sein. Dann heißt es: Cittaslow", in: *brand eins* (08/2007), Hamburg: brand eins Verlag, 2007, pp. 130–137

Weiner, M. F.; Cullum, C. M.; Rosenberg, R. N. and Honig, L. S.: "Aging and Alzheimer's disease: lessons from the Nun Study", in: *Gerontologist* 1998; 38: pp. 5–6

Welter, R. and Hürlimann, M. and Hürlimann-Siebke, K.: *Gestaltung von Betreuungseinrichtungen für Menschen mit Demenzerkrankungen*, Zurich: Demenzplus Hürlimann + Welter, 2006

World Health Organization: *Dementia – A Public Health Priority*, Geneva, 2012

Acknowledgements

Many people have contributed to the development of this book. Prof. Ursula Lehr (Germany), Prof. Mary Marshall (Great Britain), Dr. Radha S. Murthy (India), Prof. Elisabeth Steinhagen-Thiessen (Germany), Richard Taylor, PHD (USA) and Dr. John Zeisel (USA) all offered valuable input as we were developing the idea for this book.

We would like to thank all the authors who have contributed to this book for sharing their expertise and experience from many different disciplines and their perspectives on the subject of architecture and dementia. Likewise, we would like to thank all the architects and their clients as well as the artists, institutions and private collectors from all over the world who have generously allowed us to show their projects, plans, photographs and works of arts in the documentation and accompanying illustrations.

In particular, we would like to thank our editor, Christel Kapitzki, who throughout the process of working on this book offered advice and assistance and shared her extensive experience of developing book publications.

In addition, we would like to thank all the institutions and companies who, like us, are interested in architecture and dementia and in contributing to improving the sensory experience of architecture.

BOS
Best Of Steel

BOS Best Of Steel is the leading manufacturer of steel frames in Europe and has been producing steel and stainless steel frames for doors and windows for over 45 years. With our team of qualified architects, we can help you find the best standard product or develop a tailor-made solution to match your needs.
Design, function and sustainability for all areas of your building.

mauser
möbel die mitdenken

Furnishing systems for the health care sector Mauser Einrichtungssysteme manufactures complete furnishing systems for the living, communal and work areas of care homes and rehabilitation and social centres. The company assists its clients from the initial idea to the fully furnished property and provides a complete range of services from development to manufacture and installation.

Residenz-Gruppe Bremen

The Residenz-Gruppe Bremen is one of the 20 largest private nursing care providers in Germany. Beyond the portfolio of 35 nursing care facilities the company operates a nursing service and an acute care hospital and a rehabilitation clinic. The group's managing director, Rolf Specht, was named Bremen's businessman of the year in 2010.

Hans Sauer Stiftung

The Hans Sauer Stiftung (a foundation) has been active for more than 25 years in the support and funding of research and invention. Initiated by the benefactor and inventor Hans Sauer (1923–1996), the foundation supports technical and social innovations that are of obvious ecological and social value.

Waldmann W
ENGINEER OF LIGHT.

Waldmann develops high-quality and efficient lighting systems for the industrial, office and health care sectors as well as medical systems for UV-phototherapy. The company can draw on more than ten years' experience and expertise in the effect of light on the physical and mental well-being of people.

ARTHUR WASER GRUPPE
Wertschriften|Immobilien|Beteiligungen

The Arthur Waser Gruppe manages its own property portfolio with particular focus on commercial and industrial real estate. It acquires holdings in companies and invests in securities. In 1999 the Arthur Waser Stiftung was established as a foundation to support cultural and social projects.

Illustration credits

P. 13: Pius Fox
P. 14: Asim Waqif
P. 16: Feddersen Architekten, photographer: David Brandt, Dresden
P. 17: Feddersen Architekten
P. 18: Photographie Luc Pagés
P. 19: Christel Kapitzki
P. 21: Alvar Aalto Museum
P. 22: (above) photographer: Sascha J. Hardt
THEATER DER KLÄNGE
Figur und Klang im Raum (1993)
Direction: J.U. Lensing
Costume design: Kerstin Uebachs, Caterina Di Fiore
Actors:
Yellow: Kerstin Hörner
Red: Jacqueline Fischer
Blue: Heiko Seidel
www.theater-der-klaenge.de
P. 22: (below) Stiftung Bauhaus Dessau
P. 23: Stiftung Bauhaus Dessau
P. 25: Irina Lucius
P. 26: Klaus Frahm
P. 27: Sigrid Sandmann
P. 29: Friederike Tebbe
P. 30: (above) Stefan Müller
P. 30: (below) Feddersen Architekten, photographer: Ronald Grunert-Held
P. 31: Stefan Müller
P. 33–35: Bernasconi + Partner Architekten AG
P. 37–41: Michel Feinen/ witry & witry
P. 43: Steinprinz, Wuppertal
P. 44: (above) Leniger, Paderborn
P. 44: (below) Großkemm + Richard Architekten Innenarchitekten
P. 45: (above) Leniger, Paderborn
P. 45: (below) Großkemm/ Richard Architekten Innenarchitekten
P. 46–47: Leniger, Paderborn
P. 49: VG Bildkunst (for Michal Rovner)

P. 51: Daniela Tobias (performance by Avi Kaiser)
P. 53: Pius Fox
P. 54: Allessandro Lupi (artist), photographer: Guido Castagnoli
P. 57: ter Hell
P. 58: Bernd Brach
P. 60–61 : Annina Gähwiler
P. 63: Tamara Kvesitadze (artist), photographer: Daro Sulakauri (representation in Germany: Galerie Kornfeld Kunsthandel GmbH & Co. KG)
P. 64 : Archivio Gianni Colombo
P. 67: Claudia Thoelen
P. 68 : (above) Elisabeth Heinemann
P. 68 : (below) Bernasconi + Partner Architekten AG
P. 77: Michael Uhlmann
P. 78: Feddersen Architekten
P. 81–82: Jan Oelker
P. 84–85: Mauser Einrichtungssysteme GmbH & Co. KG
P. 87: VG Bildkunst (for Werner Heldt)
P. 89: Andrea Rosen Gallery (for Andrea Zittel)
P. 91: Pius Fox
P. 92: Iwan Baan
P. 94–95: FAR frohn&rojas
P. 96: Atelier Bow-Wow
P. 97: Mette Ramsgard Thomsen (CITA), Ayelet Karmon (Shenkar College of Engineering and Design), Dr. Eyal Sheffer and Ami Cang (Knitting Lab, Textile Design Department), Tzach Harari (Robotics Lab), Yair Reshef (Interactive)
P. 98–99: Iwan Baan
P. 100: Feddersen Architekten, photographer: Michael Holz
P. 101: (above) Johan Fowelin
P. 101: (below) Feddersen Architekten, Photographer: Ronald Grunert-Held
P. 103: photographer: Lasse Ryberg, SHJWORKS (project)
P. 104: Perkins Eastman Architects
P. 105: Milroy and McAleer Photography
P. 107: Feddersen Architekten, photographer: Ronald Grunert-Held

P. 108–109: Olaf Becker
P. 111: Insa Lüdtke
P. 113: Feddersen Architekten, photographer: Ronald Grunert-Held
P. 115: Johan Fowelin
P. 116: Plan: Marge Arkitekter AB
P. 117: Johan Fowelin
P. 119–120: Photographer: Jörn Lehmann/Schwerin, Plans: Dipl.-Ing. Architekt Erich Schneekloth & Partner
P. 121: Photographer: Jörn Lehmann/Schwerin
P. 123–125: Asim Waqif
P. 127: Private collection, Se Ra Park (artist)
P. 128: Rudolf Steiner Archiv
P. 130: Feddersen Architekten, photographer: Ronald Grunert-Held
P. 132: Beth Tauke (left), William Helm (right)
P. 135: Pius Fox
P. 136: The Walters Art Museum
P. 138: Steffen Großmann
P. 139: (above) carlier | gebauer (German representation for Julie Mehretu)
P. 139: (below) Großkemm/ Richard Architekten Innenarchitekten
P. 140–141: Steffen Großmann
P. 142: Photographer: Christa Lachenmaier, Cologne, ASTOC Architects and Planners, Cologne (architects)
P. 143–145: Photographer: Mischa Erben, heri&salli (project)
P. 147: Insa Lüdtke
P. 148: (above) Insa Lüdtke
P. 148: (below) Harms Wulf Landschaftsarchitekten
P. 149: Photographer: Ronald Grunert-Held, Harms Wulf Landschaftsarchitekten
P. 151: Dipl.-Ing. Architekt Erich Schneekloth & Partner, photographer Jörg Lehmann/ Schwerin
P. 152–153: Beat Bühler
P. 155–157: Jörg Lammert GEROTEKTEN
P. 159–163: Feddersen Architekten
P. 165: Photographer: Jesús Granada

P. 166: Plan: Carroquino Finner Arquitectos:
P. 166: Photographer: Jesús Granada
P. 167: Plan: Carroquino Finner Arquitectos
P. 168–169: Photographer: Jesús Granada
P. 171–175: Miguel Arruda
P. 177: Dementia Village Architects
Taalstraat 112
5261 BH VUGHT
Netherlands
T: +31 73 658 70 70
W: www.dementiavillage.com
E: live@dementiavillage.com
KvK : 17145768
P. 178: (above) Insa Lüdtke
P. 178: (below) Dementia Village Architects, www.dementiavillage.com
P. 179–181: Dementia Village Architects, www.dementiavillage.com
P. 182–183: Eleni Kolovou
P. 185: Pius Fox
P. 186: Beat Bühler
P. 195: 100% interior Sylvia Leydecker, photographer: Reinhard Rosendahl
P. 196: 100% interior Sylvia Leydecker, photographer: Karin Hessmann
P. 197: Feddersen Architekten, photographer: Reinhard Görner
P. 198–199: sander.hofrichter architekten GmbH
P. 201–202: Margherita Lazzati
P. 204–207: Anagram Architects
P. 209: Meinhard von Gerkan/ gmp Architekten
P. 210 (above): Heiner Leiska Photography
P. 210 (below): HG Esch Photography
P. 211: Marcus Bredt Fotografie
P. 212: Steffen Großmann
P. 213: Kunst- und Kulturstiftung Opelvillen Rüsselsheim, photographer: Frank Möllenberg
P. 215: Michael Uhlmann
P. 217: Michael Uhlmann